LIVES &
LEGACIES

Duke Ellington

SERIES EDITOR: BARBARA LEAH ELLIS

JANNA TULL STEED

Duke Ellington

A Spiritual Biography

*For Jackie and Graham,
with all best wishes —
Janna Tull Steed*

A Crossroad Book
The Crossroad Publishing Company
New York

The Crossroad Publishing Company
370 Lexington Avenue, New York, NY 10017

First published in 1999 by The Crossroad Publishing Company

LIBRARY OF CONGRESS CATALOGING-IN-PUBLICATION DATA
Steed, Janna Tull
Duke Ellington : a spiritual biography / written by Janna Tull Steed.
p. cm. – (Lives & legacies)
Includes bibliographical references.
ISBN 0-8245-2351-2 (hc.)
1. Ellington, Duke, 1899-1974. 2. Jazz musicians—United States
Biography. I. Title. II. Series.
ML410.E44 S74   1999
781.65'092—dc21
[B]   99-42719

Printed in the United States of America
Set in Janson
Designed by SCRIBES Editorial
Cover design by Kaeser and Wilson Design Ltd.

Acknowledgements are made to the following sources:

John Edward Hasse, curator of American Music at the National Museum of American
History, Smithsonian Institution, and author of *Beyond Category: The Life and Genius of
Duke Ellington.* New York: Simon & Schuster, 1993.

Mark Tucker, editor, *The Duke Ellington Reader.* New York: Oxford University Press,
Inc., 1933.

HEAVEN (from Second Sacred Concert)
By Duke Ellington
Copyright 1968 (Renewed) Famous Music Corp. and Tempo Music, Inc.
Used by permission.

SOLITUDE, by Duke Ellington, Eddie DeLange and Irving Mills
Copyright 1934 (Renewed) EMI Mills Music, Inc., Famous Music Corporation and
Scarsdale Music Corporation in U.S.A.
All Rights outside U.S.A. controlled by EMI Mills Music, Inc.
All Rights Reserved. Used by permission.
WARNER BROS. PUBLICATIONS U.S. INC., Miami, FL 33014

1 2 3 4 5 6 7 8 9 10 03 02 01 00 99

for Edward Kennedy Ellington
and for the One who knows all our stories and songs,
beginning to end

CONTENTS

Duke Ellington

Duke Ellington, Paris, 1960. (Photo © Herman Leonard)

1

Recapitulation

In sweet music is such art,
Killing care and grief of heart. . . .
—William Shakespeare

HELD BACK BY POLICE CORDONS, more than two thousand people were standing outside the Cathedral of St. John the Divine in Manhattan on Memorial Day, May 27, 1974, as loudspeakers broadcast a service in progress within those massive and towering Gothic walls. New York City's largest house of worship was packed that afternoon with a congregation of ten thousand people, among them enough musicians to have staged a marathon performance of stellar quality. But the man who had brought them together for this occasion was being mourned and eulogized. The crowd "ranged through the whole human colour scale, from the most purple black to the most pallid white," Alistair Cooke wrote later that week. "Every pew was filled, and the aisles were choked. . . . And when the ten thousand people inside were asked to stand and pray, there was a vast rustling sound as awesome, it struck me, as that of the several million bats whooshing out of the Carlsbad Caverns in New Mexico at the first blush of twilight."[1]

This mass of people had come to honor Edward Kennedy Ellington, known around the globe simply as "the Duke." The origin of that nickname, given to him in his youth, has been

3

traced in distinctly different anecdotes. What remains is the impression that the mature man seemed titled by divine right and the pure strength of his singular sense of self and vocation. Ellington's claim to nobility won widespread acceptance because of his mastery of the art of jazz—and the grandeur of his humanity—in all its complexity and contradictions. Both he and his orchestra, which he led for roughly half a century, had become an American institution and an international treasure by the time Ellington died on May 24, 1974. He was seventy-five years old, and for sixty of those years he had been making music.

Duke wrote his first composition, "Soda Fountain Rag," as a fourteen-year-old schoolboy imitating the ragtime piano players in his hometown of Washington, D.C. As a teenager, he began substituting for established players. Soon he was booking his own engagements, and by 1923 he was the pianist-arranger in a five-piece dance band formed by a group of musician friends. New York City beckoned, and, after several false starts, The Washingtonians—as they called themselves in those years—were recording and playing regularly in their new home base. The addition of several "hot jazz" players and Ellington's ascendance to leadership of the band brought into existence a unique ensemble whose performance innovations shaped jazz in its early years and beyond.

The Duke Ellington Jazz Orchestra played at the Cotton Club from December of 1927 to February of 1931. By that time, the band was an orchestra of about ten pieces and carried Ellington's name, although the Cotton Club owners publicized it as a "jungle band." Network broadcasts from Harlem's premier nightclub (which featured "colored" entertainers for an exclusively white audience) brought the band's distinctive sound into the nation's homes. Recordings and sheet music were successfully marketed here and overseas by Ellington's business partner and occasional lyricist, Irving Mills; and, in 1930, recordings of "Mood Indigo" (originally titled "Dreamy Blues") established Ellington's worldwide fame. In his early filmwork in Hollywood, Ellington avoided the demeaning or stereotypical roles then foisted on African Americans and, consequently, became a cultural hero. He returned from a successful European tour in 1933 with critical accolades ringing in his ears; abroad he and his sidemen were treated as artists of the first rank. This experience strengthened his resolve to continue on the creative path he had been following.

Ellington's life paralleled the development of jazz. He was growing up when the traditions of European classical music, and marching bands were alchemically mixed with the syncopations of ragtime and stride piano; with the instruments of marching bands; and with the musical elements from Negro work songs, spirituals, and the blues. The amalgam became a new and uniquely American music—a fusion of European and African elements. Ellington remained idiosyncratically himself, never trendy but always modern, through the various permutations of jazz during his lifetime: swing, bebop, hot, cool, progressive, third-stream, modal, free jazz, avant-garde, fusion. "He swung before there was swing, and he bopped before there was bop. He was fourth stream before there was third stream! And he did it all with trend-setting style."[2]

While his innovations served as a foundation for jazz and still influence musicians of all kinds, Ellington's popular songs have for decades been an integral part of the American musical landscape. Ellington composed in a collaborative style, often incorporating contributions of individual band members, but his was the artistic imagination that poured forth a steady stream of jazz masterpieces and memorable songs. "Caravan," "Solitude," "I Let a Song Go Out of My Heart," "Do Nothin' Till You Hear From Me," "Prelude to a Kiss," "In a Mellotone," "Sophisticated Lady," "Satin Doll," "Don't

Get Around Much Anymore," "I'm Beginning to See the Light," and "I Got It Bad and That Ain't Good" are among his popular hits. "Take the 'A' Train," which served as the orchestra's theme song from the early 1940s on, was written by Ellington's chief collaborator, Billy Strayhorn. A gifted composer in his own right, Strayhorn was an important influence in Ellington's ever-expanding creativity.

Although Duke was without question a jazz musician, he often expressed distaste for the word "jazz," unless it was simply defined as "freedom of expression."[3] He was known to say, "I don't write jazz; I write Negro folk music." He detested what he called "categorization"—any label or descriptive term that would be a confining box. He adopted the phrase "beyond category" as his highest complement, and now that phrase is used to describe Ellington himself. (Both John Edward Hasse's 1993 biography and the Smithsonian Institution's traveling exhibit took this phrase as their titles.) Certainly Ellington's creativity broke through the confines of jazz standards and popular dance tunes. He also wrote orchestral suites, tone poems, impressionistic piano solos, musical revues, movie scores, reinterpretations of works by Peter Tchaikovsky and Edward Grieg, a comic opera, and music for plays by Shakespeare and T.S. Eliot. In the last decade of his life, he wrote many pieces for performance in Sacred Concerts.

The Duke possessed an eccentrically elegant sense of style. Whether he was designing his own clothes or giving instructions about one of his conglomerate desserts, the project was an artistic exercise. He had a rich, distinctive voice with an accent vaguely reminiscent of a southern aristocrat of British origin, even when he was "talking jive." Both on and off stage, he had a commanding presence and engaging manner. He used them to create his own universe, one in which others orbited around him, whether to their detriment or enrichment—or both—is debatable. Despite certain affectations and a virtually impenetrable defense against intimacy, he charmed fans and prompted love for himself within many different circles of family, friends, and band members. "We do love you madly," was his standard closing line, and he learned to say it in many languages. This was repeated to every audience, wherever gathered. The sites of his performances included college gymnasiums, the White House and foreign palaces, Las Vegas casinos, Elks Club halls, Manhattan night clubs, civic centers in America's heartland, bull-fighting arenas in Spain, concert halls, the Harlem Jazzmobile and the London Palladium, outdoor jazz festivals on both coasts, and houses of worship—from a Jewish temple in Beverly Hills to a Catholic basilica in Barcelona.

In the early years, when the jazz venues were Prohibition-era speak-easies, Ellington was a stylistic innovator in a new music that was often vilified as a corrupting influence. Jazz was even called the "devil's music," an association that persisted for many years in the black church. Later Duke's orchestra performed in symphony halls and cathedrals and on goodwill tours abroad for the U.S. Department of State. Throughout his career Ellington was a symbol of black achievement, making his case for human equality and kinship with ironic understatement and unassailable aplomb. By the time of his death, he had received numerous honorary doctorates, prestigious medals bestowed by heads of state, and applause from people of every race, rank, and station.

Through the years his artistry received high praise from such musical luminaries as Igor Stravinsky, Darius Milhaud, Percy Grainger, Leopold Stowkowski, Aaron Copland, and Gunther Schuller. Yet in 1965 the Pulitzer Prize board declined to endorse its music committee's recommendation to give Ellington a special citation for his overall contribution to American music. In the aftermath of an uproar over this rejection, the sixty-six-year-old Ellington responded with trenchant irony: "Fate is being kind to me. Fate doesn't want me to be too famous too young." Subsequently he was showered with honorary degrees, the Presidential Medal of Freedom, and the highest awards from countries such as France and Ethiopia.

Both the orchestra and Ellington's own energies were somewhat diminished during the last few years of his career, but Ellington remained creative until the very end of his life. Even while suffering from cancer in an advanced stage, the Maestro continued touring; the band's last overseas trip under his leadership included the October 1973 premiere of the Third Sacred Concert in Westminster Abbey on United Nations Day and a Royal Command Performance for Queen Elizabeth II. In addition to European appearances, the orchestra played in Zambia and Ethiopia, where the musicians were received like visiting royalty.

Duke Ellington died in the early morning hours May 24. That night CBS News interrupted its regular programming for a one-hour special report, "A Tribute to Duke Ellington." In its May 25 front-page story, *The New York Times* called him a "master of music" and "America's foremost composer," and President Richard Nixon issued an official statement saying that the "memory of America's greatest composer" would live worldwide for generations to come. In the days between his death and the service at St. John the Divine, the funeral home stayed open around the clock to accommodate more than sixty-five thousand people who filed by his casket. From all walks of life they came; they left tokens of affection and religious devotion in the casket; they touched and kissed the strong, tan fingers and the beloved face, now shrunken; so handsome in youth, and with age unforgettably molded into a weary dignity.

Edward Kennedy Ellington was born in Washington, D.C., April 29, 1899. Seven years earlier, construction had begun on

The Duke Ellington Orchestra in 1935. (Courtesy Duke Ellington Collection, Archives Center, National Museum of American History, Smithsonian Institution.)

Lighted marquee featuring the Ellington band, 1940s. (Courtesy Stanley Dance and Helen Oakley Dance Collection, Yale Music Library)

the Episcopal Cathedral on Manhattan's Upper West Side, not far from the Harlem addresses Ellington would later call home. He was not an Episcopalian, but the Cathedral Church of St. John the Divine had hosted a performance of Ellington's First Sacred Concert and then commissioned the Second Sacred Concert, performed January 19, 1968. During the last decade of his life, Ellington had formed close associations with leading members of the clergy, including the Episcopal bishops of the Diocese of New York, and had begun to think of himself as part of an ecumenical team. His work of writing texts and music for these concerts took on the quality of a mission for him. Three concerts were premiered at major houses of worship; more than one hundred other performances were given in churches and other settings in the United States and abroad. In various ways he repeatedly indicated that the Sacred Concerts were of supreme importance to him.

At that Memorial Day funeral, then, Ellington was remembered not only as a great musician, jazz pioneer, and composer "beyond category." He was also remembered as a man of faith. Stanley Dance—record producer, jazz critic, and writer as well as longtime friend—was asked by Ellington's son Mercer to deliver the eulogy. His moving tribute included these words:

> . . . Duke Ellington knew that what some called genius was really the exercise of gifts which stemmed from God. These gifts were those his Maker favored. The Son of God said, "Fear not. Go out and teach all nations. Proclaim the good news to all. . . ." And Duke knew the good news was Love, of God and his fellow men. He proclaimed the message in his Sacred Concerts, grateful for an opportunity to acknowledge something of which he stood in awe, a power he considered above his human limitations. He firmly

believed what the mother he worshipped also believed, that he had been blessed at birth. He reached out to people with his music and drew them to himself. . . .

It is Memorial Day, when those who died for the free world are properly remembered. Duke Ellington never lost faith in this country, and he served it well. His music will go on serving it for years to come.[4]

The Right Reverend Harold Wright, suffragan bishop of the Episcopal Diocese of New York, presided over the funeral. The Reverend John Gensel, Lutheran pastor to the New York jazz community, along with members of the Cathedral staff, took a leading role. Father Norman O'Connor and Father Gerald Pocock of Montreal also took part in the liturgy, along with Father John Sanders, who had left Ellington's band to enter the Roman Catholic priesthood. Joining the Ellington family and thousands of other mourners were Pearl Bailey, who came representing President Richard Nixon; Benny Goodman; Buddy Rich; Sy Oliver; Jonah Jones; former and present members of the Ellington orchestra and other great jazz bands. Sitting with his wife, near Ellington family members, was Count Basie, whose friendship with Ellington spanned five decades. "Basie never stopped crying. He sat there and wept," said a friend of Ellington. "He never stopped crying."[5]

McHenry Boatwright (Ellington's brother-in-law) sang "The Lord's Prayer" in operatic style. Joe Williams and Earl Hines had flown in from Nevada. Williams sang Ellington's nostalgic description of his loving family, "Heritage," and Hines created a highly original medley of "Mood Indigo," "Solitude," "I Got It Bad and That Ain't Good," and "Satin Doll." Jazz pianist Mary Lou Williams and a bassist played Larry Gales's composition "Holy Ghost," and Brock Peters, who had sung in the New York presentations of Ellington's First Sacred Concert, recited appropriate lines by a poet from the West Indies. He also performed, a cappella, a song never before publicly performed or recorded, one of several pieces Ellington had written for an unproduced stage play. Herb Martin's lyric for "They Say" was based on a South African folk tale about people becoming stars when they die.[6]

Accompanied only by Billy Taylor at the piano, Ella Fitzgerald sang the traditional "Just a Closer Walk with Thee." At the end of a poignant, prayerful interpretation of "Solitude," her voice broke ever so slightly as she took the melody higher for the final phrase, "In my solitude I'm praying, 'Dear Lord above, bring back my love.'" Cathedral organist Alec Wyton improvised on Billy Strayhorn's haunting "Lotus Blossom," and the entire congregation joined in singing the triumphant hymn "Onward, Christian Soldiers." Musicians who didn't know all the words scatted through the verses. None of Ellington's orchestra members played; it was too emotional for them. Ray Nance, Ellington's violinist, was the only one to perform. He was paired with pianist Brooks Kerr for "Come Sunday" preceding the dismissal.

After Ellington's death, his sister Ruth had called Alice Babs, the Swedish soprano who had sung in Ellington's Sacred Concerts, to ask that she perform two pieces he had requested for his funeral: "Almighty God Has Those Angels" and "Heaven," visions of the afterlife from the Second Sacred Concert. "I knew that I would fall apart," Alice said, and she had to decline; but she made arrangements to fly over for the service from her home in Spain. A tape from the original performance was hastily pulled together, but few people knew about this. During the recessional, as the cortege made its way down the long center aisle, the unmistakable sound of Ellington's strong fingers playing a delicate piano introduction drifted down from that vaulted ceiling. The cavernous space was then filled by the pure, clear tones of Alice's voice, followed by the warm and plaintive sound of alto saxophonist Johnny Hodges, interpreting Ellington's chromatic evocation of "Heaven." Hodges had died in 1970. Babs was in the congregation, honoring the Maestro in voiceless grief; unprepared for this final musical offering, she almost collapsed. Hearing the tape recording over the Cathedral sound system left other stunned mourners overwhelmed with tearful emotion.[7]

Even at his own funeral, then, Edward Kennedy Ellington had the last word and the final note. It was as if, with almost whimsical reassurance, he were saying "Amen" to the prayers of family, friends, and fans. He seemed to be blessing them, as his mother had told him he was blessed, and reminding them—once again—of the ultimate destination.

> *Heaven, my dream*
> *Heaven, divine*
> *Heaven, supreme*
> *Heaven combines*
> *Every sweet and pretty thing*
> *Life would love to bring:*
> *Heavenly Heaven to be*
> *Is just the ultimate degree to be.*

Duke on stage. (Courtesy Dance Collection, Yale Music Library)

2

The Road Taken

Every artist writes his own autobiography.
—*Havelock Ellis*

EDWARD KENNEDY ELLINGTON RECEIVED the first honorary doctorate of music given by Berklee College of Music in Boston, a pioneering institution in jazz education that Ellington had worked with for many years. After the ceremonies Duke played his own reception, tossing off "Satin Doll" and "Take the 'A' Train" and honoring requests for "Sophisticated Lady" and the Fats Waller tune "Honeysuckle Rose." Two vocalists in the Ellington organization joined him at the piano. Nell Brookshire promised to "Love You Madly," right or wrong. Toney Watkins, a regular contributor to the Sacred Concerts, delivered "Come Sunday"—in Hebrew. Even the Duke himself broke into song after humming and grunting along on the bridge of "Baby, You Can't Miss," a tune he had only recently introduced. This "hip" four-word title summed up his earlier speech to the Class of 1971:

> I'm writing a book right now about how I got where I am here today, and it's a rather simple book, because I'm not really a book writer. I go about it in a way that says . . . a very pretty lady and a very handsome man got married and God blessed

15

them with a lovely, little baby boy—eight pounds, eight ounces. They cradled, cuddled him, pampered him, spoiled him until he was about eight years old. Finally they let his feet touch the ground, and he ran out into the front yard, out the gate, out in the middle of the street. And somebody said, "Hey, get out of the middle of the street!" And I went to the other side of the street—oh, that was me, incidentally. I got to the other side of the street. Somebody said, "Up this way, Edward." And so I went up there. When we got up there, somebody said, "Take a left-hand turn." And we got to the next corner; "Take a right-hand, go straight ahead. You can't miss it.

Well, this is really the history of my career. . . . It's just what Dr. Berks was talking about. People who are prepared and have acquired all the foundations to go out into the world to do this thing . . . should not be discouraged by one simple little failure or the loss of an opportunity. You can never tell, because it's usually at a point when you least expect it, that something really big happens. And I think that's about all I can say to the ladies and gentlemen of the graduating class. . . . My career has been just one long parade of meeting people who have directed me, wonderful people. . . . Actually the book is just an opportunity for a lot of name-dropping. It shows you that . . . such a large percentage of it is luck, and particularly with me.[1]

Duke was prone to affectations of modesty. He liked to spin humorous stories to entertain without revealing much. But in his remarks at Berklee, he was saying more than what shines on the glittery surface. Underneath the "Ellington jive" is some truth he wanted to convey. He knew about discouragement and failure. He had overcome great obstacles to do what he loved and what the world loved him for doing. He could (and did) take pride in his fame and his talents. It took personal courage, ingenuity, stamina, and strength of will to reach the pinnacle of his seventy-plus years. He had stood alone and had things come out all right, he told one writer in 1944. He attributed this strength to his feeling of being "God's son." Religion had been proved to him, he said, by the way things had happened in his life.[2] So Duke's story about the little boy dutifully following directions as he explored his world is not just a fanciful allegory. Ellington expected to be providentially guided: If someone comes along, better pay attention. He might turn out to be Sonny Greer, Harry Carney, or Billy Strayhorn. If Johnny Hodges is playing a three-note warm-up riff in the confusion of rehearsals, listen. That could be "I'm Beginning to See the Light" in gestation. If a scheduled arrival or departure is delayed, don't pick a fight with the Power of the Universe. Just wait and see what blessing might come under the guise of inconvenience.

The fable Duke spun for these young musicians at Berklee did indeed end up in a collection of his memoirs, written with the help of his friend Stanley Dance. *Music Is My Mistress* was published two years later. As an autobiography the book seems to be lightweight fare. There are idealized memories of childhood and adolescence, descriptions of memorable meals, and warm tributes to people Duke had met along the way. The book loosely follows the lines of a theatrical program organized into Prologue, Acts, and Epilogue, with *dramatis felidae* interspersed throughout. In "Seeing God" and "The Mirrored Self" Ellington offers some conclusions about his introspections. Tucked among other topics are philosophical reflections and little nuggets of impassioned thought about art, music, faith, human nature. Ellington is a prolific thinker as well as a prolific composer. Writing about the misleading effect of the style of *Music Is My Mistress*, one Ellington discographer offered a precise observation:

"What we in fact have is a literary version of the favorite Ellington trick, that of presenting something of real substance in the guise of a happy little entertainment."[3]

Sharing his conclusions metaphorically or in an offhand manner, Duke offers at least a glimpse of his many selves. But there is little offhand in the twenty-four pages devoted to the Sacred Concerts. Ellington inserted all the titles of pieces, with the full texts of lyrics, written for the Second Sacred Concert. There are pictures of Baby Laurence tap dancing and Toney Watkins singing at a performance in Orange, France; one of Ellington posing with Pastor John Gensel; others of Duke and the orchestra in packed sanctuaries. The program from the premiere at St. John the Divine is also reproduced. The one who had for decades been called the Maestro, by then was calling himself "God's messenger boy." The Sacred Concerts, he said, were an opportunity to make an offering, and he proudly described how people had responded to them. In laconic responses to an imaginary interviewer in the Epilogue, Ellington said that one of his problems was answering to his "other selves." He had to answer to his better self in his music, he said. But the work of his "best self" was writing and playing the sacred music, keeping himself honest with himself—and praying.[4]

Ellington also chose music from the Second Sacred Concert when he was asked to donate an original manuscript to the archives of The New York Public Library for the Performing Arts at Lincoln Center. These manuscripts reveal how Duke characteristically notated his scores with names of individual players, instead of scoring for parts such as first trumpet, second trumpet, etc. One margin contains the name and telephone number of the dancer he wanted to perform; another, a list of religious leaders whom he considered partners in an ecumenical mission. From the 1965 Concert of Sacred Music performed in San Francisco's

Grace Cathedral, until his death, Ellington and his orchestra presented more than one hundred concerts of his sacred music around the world. In one radio interview, Duke said the concerts were the most important thing in his life, and in both his speaking and his writing he repeatedly identified the Sacred Concerts as his most important work or statement.

It's remarkable that Duke made these claims. He resisted ranking or categorizing his own work. Music wasn't "work" to him anyway; it was "dreaming." Asked to choose his favorite recording or composition, he would talk about the one he was about to write, the dream that was still "a-pippin'." Besides that, the sacred music seems at first glance to be a strange choice. Few Ellington experts judge these forty-odd pieces as a whole to be exceptional, unless as a kind of novelty, when they are placed alongside other work. Did Duke really rank them above "Daybreak Express," "Reminiscing in Tempo," "Old Man Blues," "Creole Rhapsody," "Flamingo," "Mood Indigo," "Ko-Ko," "Concerto for Cootie," which he or others singled out as favorites?

Ellington loved to play with words. He chose his words carefully, but sometimes to obfuscate, to project an image, to flatter —or to discourage further conversation by creating a verbal smokescreen. Ellington did not call the sacred music his best *music*, but, rather, his most important work, his most significant statement. The significance of his "statement" had as much to do with the whole performance context—worship setting, participants, congregation, cultural factors—as it did with the music and words per se. As Stanley Dance said in his eulogy, Ellington knew that what some called genius was really the exercise of gifts from God. Yet the opportunity to present this music in a consecrated space added a new dimension of awareness. If he didn't go about it with the right spirit, he said, those beautiful colored windows would come crashing down on his head.

Ellington didn't propose bringing what he sometimes called his "noise" within consecrated spaces. He didn't knock on the church's door. Representatives of the church had invited him to perform his music under awe-inspiring Gothic arches, with the beauty of tapestry and stained glass, with fine sculpture and wood carving and sanctuary appointments all around. Still, Ellington expressed some trepidation about how his offering would be received by others and even by the one he called the "great God of Love." He said he had to consider whether he was "eligible" to makes his statement about God. "That's the true Duke," said Barry Ulanov, an early biographer. "That's his way of sort of dodging around it. And it's genuine. He really had to consider that always. Deep down he was really a modest human being. He had to be led into this, although he certainly went willingly once the door was open. . . . I never talked to him about this, but I'm not at all sure that he believed he was worthy."[5] When Ellington and the churches began this venture, there were skeptical reactions toward both. Some assumed the churches wanted the publicity and Ellington wanted the respectability. Many who knew Duke or who avidly admire his music dismiss the religious side of Ellington as one of the mirrors employed to protect his privacy.

His claims to be a man of faith who regularly prayed and read his Bible seem contradicted by his image. He personified urbane sophistication combined with an elemental sensuality. He had done more than his share of hard drinking and womanizing—but neither was he averse to enhancing his reputation by embellishments and inventions. Once when he was characteristically late for an appearance at a major hotel, he faced a hostile audience and won them over with a fictional explanation for his delay. "Forgive me, ladies and gentleman—but, believe me, if you had seen her, you would understand." After a split second of indecision, the appreciative laughter began. They were all in the palm of his hand. He sometimes spoke with amusement about the propensities of writers to look for decadence in jazz musicians, convinced that it was a necessary ingredient for the mysterious and, to their minds, somewhat primitive process of making jazz.

Throughout his life Ellington made his worldliness a part of his public persona and usually kept his spirituality hidden. Although he jealously shielded his private life from the press, part of his public persona was that of the great lover of women, and his reputation was apparently well deserved. He was known as a generous and considerate man, but also as one who put his own needs first; and he was a master at getting what he wanted. He was a connoisseur of beauty, except that he saw beauty even where others did not, and his appetites were huge. No asceticism or simple living for the Duke. No poverty either, although it was not money itself he wanted but the means to live in high style and be generous with others. The cross around his neck signified his faith tradition, but he wasn't known to attend religious services regularly or identify himself with a particular denomination of the Christian church. Given his schedule and style of life, can he really have read the Bible through several times as he claimed?

Judging from the many translations and versions of Bibles acquired by the Smithsonian from Ellington's estate, he was quite a reader of such material. The lyrics of the Sacred Concert music are infused with biblical texts, language, metaphors, and images, although Ellington certainly paraphrased ideas in his own idiosyncratic fashion. His familiarity with the Bible is revealed in a story told by jazz singer Jon Hendricks, whom Duke asked to perform in the First Sacred Concert, in part because of Hendricks's religious background and convictions. Before that event, Duke was discussing with Jon his plan to include vocal scatting and tap dance in the program. When Jon expressed some reservations, Duke picked up the well-worn Bible in his dressing room and immediately found the passage in II Samuel from which he took the lyrics "David Danced Before the Lord."[6] Don George once walked in on Ellington in a small room alone and deep in prayer one night. George, whose memoir of Ellington largely consists of sexual escapades, found the intensity of the witnessed experience so overwhelming that he, for the very first time, was brought to his knees in prayer.

Barry Ulanov traveled with the band while working on his biography of Ellington, published in 1946. He learned a lot about the day-to-day life of jazz musicians as he gathered the material for his book. Yet he was not surprised when, twenty years later, Ellington presented his first Sacred Concert, even though the concept was daring at the time. "Nothing could have been more natural to him," he said in 1998. Even in that early work, Ulanov touched on the religious side of Duke's personality. "That was because I was so knocked out by what I'd seen of it," he said. "And maybe I should have done more, but that was for different purposes. . . . There are whole encyclopedias to be written about the many sides of Ellington. It's just endless." Ellington preferred to sleep during daylight hours, and that combined with his performance schedule would seem to preclude regular church attendance. When he was back in Washington, D.C., however, he used to go to St. Matthew's Cathedral, the site of John F. Kennedy's funeral, "for inspiration."[7] Among the collection of Ellington's numerous Bibles and other religious books at the Smithsonian, there are church bulletins and clippings of newspaper columns written by well-known clergy, with underlined passages.

James Lincoln Collier suggests that the Sacred Concerts appealed to Ellington mostly because he was enamored of the idea of joining the company of the great composers who wrote masses, chorales, and oratorios. Another commonly held view is that this ten-year obsession was just an old man's effort to compensate for his indiscretions, a kind of late-life conversion and baptism. A more generous reading assumes that Ellington's faith was genuine, but that it was only later in life that he gave it much attention.

Ellington's creative art was shaped by his view of the nature of reality, and that view was basically incarnational. Understanding Ellington as an incarnationalist requires focus on his way of being, of seeing and doing things. Duke's sense of regal entitlement came from the conviction that he was "God's son." "Ellington was a godly man," said Herb Jeffries, one of his vocalists. "In his heart he was godly."[8] He thought that wisdom and joy came through the "reflection and miracle of God" in the "wonder and beauty" of the world.[9] His music, and the great titles his songs were given, indicate that he looked for, and found, wonder and beauty in the most unlikely places: "Apes and Peacocks," "Lightning Bugs and Frogs," "Harlem Air Shaft," "Eerie Moan."

Some critics and even loyal fans dismiss Ellington's sacred music as inferior compositions and pan the lyrics in particular. More positive evaluations of the sacred music usually attempt to separate the wheat from the chaff, making judgment about the relative merits of the various pieces. There are also comparisons made between the three concerts, which differ in significant ways. As a critical approach, this makes sense. But few people have examined the concerts as a last testament or as a key to the enigma of Ellington's personality and approaches to his work. At the very least, Ellington's sacred music reveals one source of the power of his earlier work. The Sacred Concerts came late in Ellington's career, but as early as the late 1920s and early 1930s some critics discerned a spiritual dimension in his music.

"Black and Tan Fantasy" and "East St. Louis Toodle-O," both co-composed with "Bubber" Miley, are singled out as exam-

The world's "hippest" reception pianist plays at Berklee College of Music reception after receiving an honorary doctorate in 1971. (Photo © Berklee College of Music, Boston)

Duke sits in with Berklee Professor Herb Pomeroy's recording band in the mid 1950s. (Photo © Berklee College of Music, Boston)

Retrospective

When he was just a young boy growing up in New York City, Barry Ulanov started listening to jazz, especially the music of Duke Ellington. Ulanov was editor of *Metronome* when he wrote his biography of Duke, with whom he had a continuing association until Ellington's death. Ulanov is MacIntosh Professor of English Emeritus at Barnard College of Columbia University and a lecturer in psychiatry and religion at Union Theological Seminary. He and his wife Ann Belford Ulanov, a Jungian analyst and professor of psychiatry and religion at Union, write books on psychology and spirituality. Ulanov believes that Ellington's faith was a natural element of his personality.

"He gave us, I believe, a testimony to what jazz offers, itself, as an incarnation of the Spirit. I can't think of a music that's more insistently human and reaching out beyond the human. And Duke isn't the only one, but I think he's about the most persuasive. . . . These people were really at the center of things. That is not the going procedure in the twentieth century; but, the fact is, we have witnesses, and they continue—God doesn't desert the world in a given century, a given decade, or even in a given year. And so in the twentieth century we still have marvelous witnesses, and I think Duke was one of the most persuasive.

"For me, he just had—you know the phrase, *anima naturalis christiana*—a naturally Christian soul. And he had it, quite apart from anything to do with his culture, anything to do with his upbringing. There was something in Duke that just gravitated to the figure of Jesus. I don't mean that he said the name often. I just mean that he understood what an incarnational religion was about. That's the substance of my conviction about Duke's religiosity.

"Duke is in some ways, in spite of the more adventurous work of some of the boppers and a lot that came later, the freest spirit we ever had in jazz. But Duke had a freedom, which was, I really believe—and I try to suggest that, without just pleading for it, in the biography—freedom of the Spirit, in the Spirit, really *in* the Spirit. He lived that way.

"When I was on the road with him . . . we'd have the briefest little discussions. But so help me they became . . . they became [pause] things like biblical commentaries. I mean, they were around issues of *presence*. Now, I'd have a very hard time, I suppose, in scholarly terms justifying this with a footnoted series of references. But, so help me, it's at least as trustworthy as anything with a whole series of *ibids* and *idems*. Because he just was plugged into the Spirit. He was an incarnationalist."[10]

ples of a remarkable compositional style in the making. Both were recorded before Ellington's band became the Cotton Club Orchestra in 1927. "East St. Louis Toodle-O" was its theme song until about 1940. Another important early composition was "Black Beauty," recorded by Ellington as a piano solo and also featured with "Black and Tan Fantasy" in the 1929 movie *Black and Tan*. R.D. Darrell, writing in 1932 for a periodical usually devoted to recordings of classical music, described how on first hearing "Black and Tan Fantasy," he was struck by its spiritual power. At first laughing at the growls and ludicrous whinnies of muted trumpet and trombone, he began to discern a wild beauty and hear haunting new tone colors. Analyzing this work and others such as "Black Beauty," Darrell concluded his article with a quote from Proust, naming Ellington as one of the great artists who "do us the service . . . of showing us what richness, what variety lies hidden and unknown to us . . . in that great black impenetrable night . . . of our soul, which we have been content to regard as valueless and waste and void."[11]

Other early compositions with spiritual meaning were "Come Sunday" (1943) and "Hymn of Sorrow" (1935). The latter piece, though never recorded by Ellington, was part of a film short released in 1935. "Come Sunday" was performed in the First Sacred Concert, but it was introduced in 1943 as a wordless spiritual theme in *Black, Brown and Beige*. Other compositions without explicit religious references are striking for their meditative mood. Msgr. John Sanders, who left the band to become a Roman Catholic priest, recalls the striking effect of Duke's playing a piano solo such as "Azure" in the middle of a blockbuster stage show. Ulanov spoke of having a similar impression. "I can think of at least a dozen occasions when I watched him, when I was with him—and in later years, when I had the feeling he was there talking to somebody, feeling somebody out. I didn't know who. There may not have been anybody who was actually physically present that he had in mind. Still it was a colloquy. It was a small conversation. Maybe it was with God. Wouldn't be off for him. He was a believer."

"The Sacred Concerts expressed his own raison d'être," Ruth Ellington Boatwright said. "We were raised as Christians; that's who we were as a family." In her view, her brother's spiritual depth was also the wellspring of his unique creativity. "The spirituality of his music is why it didn't sound like anybody else's music," she said. "The jungle music was not simply that; it expressed the frustration of blacks, male-female relationships, our basic humanity. . . . When Edward was writing music he was expressing love and the emotionality of human experience."[12]

An impressive crowd gathered in Westminster Abbey for the Third Sacred Concert on October 24, 1973, exactly seven months before Ellington's death. The Maestro accepted their welcoming applause with these words: "I'm honored, and at the moment I feel a little bit blessed on being exposed to so much beauty. And, of course, the theme of this program is mainly love. And [there are] a couple of questions in the program, too, but the first statement is love, my love. The first will be 'The Lord's Prayer' on the piano. And since this is the theme of our evening, it will not be the only one. There will be many 'Lord's Prayers,' because every man prays in his own language, and there is no language that God does not understand."[13]

The program began with Ellington's solo piano setting of "The Lord's Prayer," which has a reverent, sonorous quality. This was followed by the lush and deceptively simple ballad "My Love," sung by Alice Babs, with a reinterpretation of the melody by Harry Carney on the baritone saxophone. Love, blessing, and beauty formed a trinity of virtues for Duke Ellington. "He had a funny sense of the constancy of beauty without question,"

Ulanov said, "and then of the truth that beauty might represent, and that's where it verged on the theological. And I think the sacred services are about that."

Edward Kennedy Ellington's mother was beautiful. She blessed her son, and she loved him. So she represented this trinity in his early life. Through the years he held onto the sense of blessing she imparted to him. He found beauty wherever he looked, and he sought to apprehend its truth. When "love" became the theme of his Third Sacred Concert, that word carried associations of all he had known of earthly affection, especially the love he so fondly remembered from his early family life.

3

Washington Days

My mother groan'd, my father wept,
Into the dangerous world I leapt. . . .
—*William Blake*

FROM HIS MOTHER, Daisy Kennedy Ellington, Edward learned about heaven and God at a very early age. She conveyed wonderful impressions through her "word pictures" and poetic images. Her playing of hymns or sentimental Victorian music on the piano also affected her young son deeply. When he was about four, he burst out crying when she played "The Rosary" by Ethelbert Nevin. Daisy's teaching also gave him a sense of the worth of all people, whatever the color of their skin, "because God made them." She had a strong belief that her son's life would unfold under a smiling divine countenance. Above all else, he said, she was interested in knowing about God. So every Sunday his mother took Edward to two churches: her family's church, the Nineteenth Street Baptist, and the John Wesley A.M.E. Zion, his father's family church. The denominational differences were not made clear to Edward and didn't seem to matter. The most important thing was that they both preached God and Jesus Christ. When Edward was old enough, he was sent to Sunday School. He said it gave him a "wonderful feeling of security." Believing also gave him that. His mother would say

Young Edward displays characteristic sartorial style. (Courtesy Dance Collection, Yale Music Library)

to him, "Edward, you are blessed. You don't have anything to worry about. Edward you are blessed."[1]

On the face of it, to be born black in the United States in 1899 would suggest a life of lack and meager resources, hardly a cornucopia of blessing as most people conceive it. Such a child would be limited and even threatened by racial prejudice. The nation's capital was in many ways a southern town. The benefits of democracy and justice were withheld from its people of color; prejudice and slander went unchallenged; the social structure maintained class distinctions between and even within racial groups.

Nevertheless, there were some advantages to be enjoyed. Washington ranked at or near the top of flourishing black communities that offered opportunity and a supportive environment within the confines of its neighborhoods and institutions. The city had become a magnet for free blacks long before the Civil War, and at the time of the Emancipation Proclamation their numbers greatly exceeded those of slaves. Blacks who had been granted their freedom sought to educate themselves and improve their lives generally. Rather than eke out a living as sharecroppers or field hands in the rural South, in Washington they could obtain jobs that required various skills and paid them a living wage. Blacks of high achievement such as W.E.B. Dubois, Booker T. Washington, Frederick Douglass, Harriet Tubman, Henry T. Burleigh were examples that African Americans could both be proud of and hope to follow.

The city's black elite included well-educated persons who enjoyed positions of eminence and supported their own institutions: a black newspaper, churches, and excellent public schools staffed by persons with advanced degrees from major universities. The ministers were also essayists and poets; there were conservatory-educated musicians, and others whose professional endeavors were not confined to one setting. Howard University, an all-black school, had been founded in 1867. Its professors and graduates, including ministers, enriched the intellectual discourse within the community. Together, the churches, educational institutions, concert halls, and theatres created a rich cultural environment for the city's black population.

This was Washington in 1898, when Daisy Kennedy and James Edward Ellington (usually called J.E.) were married. Their union brought together two families whose members shared aspirations for a better life. James's family had moved north from Lincolntown, North Carolina, sometime in the late 1890s. Daisy's family had roots in Virginia. James William Kennedy, her father, was one of those who came to D.C. as a freed slave. (He was also the son of a slaveholder, according to family history.) He married Alice Williams, a woman of black and Indian ancestry. Daisy was light-skinned and had completed high school, a rare achievement then. Both her appearance and her education were an advantage in D.C.'s Negro society, where social standing was based in part on shades of skin color, as well as on education, family occupation, and refinement in speech and manners. J.E.'s father was a mulatto whose father was English and whose mother was part Indian, according to Duke's younger sister Ruth. The family makeup, as she summarized it, included African, English, Irish, and Indian—genetic elements that all were expressed in Duke's music, she said. According to Ruth, J.E. was "raised by a white doctor."

The white doctor was Middleton F. Cuthbert. J.E. worked for him in various capacities, beginning perhaps as early as age fifteen, and certainly before J.E.'s marriage to Daisy. Working first as a coachman, Duke's father eventually became a trusted and intimate member of this prominent physician's household. Not having finished the eighth grade, J.E. educated himself by reading books from Dr. Cuthbert's library. For a time in 1901, two years after Edward's birth, the young family lived at the Cuthbert residence.

J.E. served as coachman and eventually as a butler for Dr. Cuthbert. He was also called on for butlering service at the White House and catering jobs at embassies and Washington mansions. In later years J.E. was a blueprint maker for the Navy. The extended family included both sets of grandparents, many aunts, uncles, and more than two dozen cousins. These provided an emotionally nourishing circle for young Edward's coming-of-age. His parents taught him that he was no one's inferior and expected him to dress and behave in ways that would inspire respect from others. In elementary school and at the Armstrong Technical High School, he learned proper speech, good manners, and pride in his race from teachers dedicated to their students' success. Music and the other arts were valued as an essential part of one's education, a refining influence. The Ellington home, as most others at the time, included an upright parlor piano. Ellington related that his music training began after his mother saw him get accidentally hit in the head during a baseball game. Such a decision would also have been part of the genteel tradition of the times. So, for whatever reason, when he was seven or eight Edward took up piano lessons with a teacher identified as Mrs. Marietta Clinkscales.

His parents also exposed him to the considerable influence of the Baptist and A.M.E. Zion churches with which his Edward's people were associated. Black Protestants had their own perspectives on the stories found in the Christian tradition, but they understood and treasured the accounts of those persons who were blessed and divinely chosen to act as messengers and sources of blessing to others. The pantheon of heroes included leaders such as Abraham, Moses, and Joshua; kings David and Solomon; and women such as Deborah, Ruth, and Mary, the mother of Jesus. These narratives and stories were part of the air young Edward breathed. They were in pictures on the Sunday school classroom wall and in the words of hymns, spirituals, children's songs, and pageants.

To be blessed was to be a player in that long story of many chapters, begun with the creation of the world and concluded in perpetual bliss at the end of time. Whether or not a child could understand such a concept intellectually, it would become part of Edward's deepest consciousness. The stories suggested what great reversals might occur in that cosmic drama. Kings became slaves, and servants became sages. Barrenness was changed to fertility. Lions were made tame. Fire did not destroy. Small forces conquered great armies. Impassable rivers were crossed and storms did not overwhelm. Rulers were deposed, and the humble elevated. Anything was possible.

So when young Edward would announce himself as the grand and glorious Duke and have his young girl cousins pay him proper homage, he was not unlike the biblical Joseph, whose dreams portended that his brothers would one day bow before him. Edward's early avowals to win acclaim may not have been simply youthful pride and self-inflation. Given the milieu of his young life, they can be understood as his announcing a divine call to greatness.

Ellington had a precocious awareness of his own destiny, and he clearly absorbed his mother's promise of blessing. But he may also have learned from her a heightened sensitivity to life's dangers. Daisy survived the sinking of a ferry boat she was riding at a time when she was carrying Edward, a frightful experience that she told him about many times. Daisy Ellington also knew about the particular dangers of being black and male. The mother of any African-American boy lived with awareness of the threat of unprovoked attacks and race-related lynchings. There can be little doubt that as a youth Duke was rebuffed or taunted by white boys, and at that age he and his buddies must have got into interracial scraps. But in his memoirs, Ellington chose not to focus on such incidents.

However, Ellington's earliest recorded memories are of two events involving threats to life and limb. Although he wrote about both in an offhand manner, the amount of detail recalled indicates how strong and clear an impression was made at an early age. At the age of four, Edward tripped over a lawnmower, fell, and cut the fourth finger of his left hand on a piece of broken milk bottle. At about the same age, he got pneumonia. Before the discovery of penicillin, this disease was a killer of young and old, and the family must have been desperately worried. The boy became aware of the seriousness of the situation when two doctors were called in. He was so ill he couldn't speak, and his mother stayed at his bedside day and night until his fever broke. Ellington credited his mother's prayers with bringing him through.

His sister Ruth was not born until Edward was sixteen, so Edward grew up as an only child. However, his birth certificate lists him as the second child born to Daisy Kennedy Ellington and James Edward Ellington. It is not unlikely that the couple's first baby died at birth or in early infancy; her second child was spared when he was so dangerously ill. These facts may help explain the doting protection she lavished upon him and the strength of her conviction that he was especially blessed.

Throughout his life Duke structured his life around idiosyncratic fears. Windows had to be closed in all weather because he was afraid of drafts. He resisted riding on boats and, later, on airplanes, until such travel became absolutely necessary for his career. In later years there was a black bag full of medicines with Duke at all times; and whenever he had the least of symptoms, wherever in the world he was, Ellington was on the phone with his personal physician. He was wearing a brown suit the day his mother died, and he never again wore the color. When *Music Is My Mistress* was given a tan cover, Duke insisted that it be changed, and early editions had to be recalled from bookstore shelves. He avoided the color green, too, because it was the color of grass, and grass reminded him of graves, an association he said he made at the tender age of eight. He regarded thirteen as a lucky number, and Friday the thirteenth was especially propitious. In one of the many contradictions of his character, Ellington believed, like his mother, that he was blessed, and throughout his life he followed intuition and circumstance leading him along a path that seemed to him directed by divine providence. Still he carried a deep awareness of how precarious life is. He had to fashion his own defenses against dangers real and imaginary.

These opposed traits, faith versus superstition and anxiety, are one example of the contradictions of Duke's personality. Even today, people will give opposite readings of the man, perhaps because he was so multifaceted. In describing Ellington, some focus on his reticence, child-likeness, and lack of pretension. Others see flamboyance and boldness verging on exhibitionism. Ulanov attributed the strong contradictions of Duke's personality to the opposing influence of both parents. An ebullient, charming man, J.E. took his pleasures wherever he found them and was not given to worry about much of anything. Ellington said that J.E. provided his family with a sense of well-being and prosperity, even though the family lived in fourteen different residences from the year of Duke's birth to 1920, when a house was purchased.[2] Ellington recalls feeling that they lived like millionaires, with fine table settings and knickknacks that J.E. received from his employer. The senior Ellington was given to flowery language that he used in efforts to charm any woman who appeared on the scene—a habit Duke was to emulate. Daisy was beautiful, but prim and a strict disciplinarian. While J.E. played piano by ear and led a group of men in barbershop singing, Daisy read music and enjoyed playing hymns and "pretty" songs such as those by Carrie Jacobs Bond. She accepted ragtime music, but frowned on the blues, as she did on makeup and other modern styles. On the whole, the personalities of J.E. and Daisy were starkly contrasting. Daisy doted on her son, and he felt extraordinarily close to her, remaining so throughout her life. Of all the women in Duke's life, Daisy Ellington was the most important and the most beloved.

The early memories Duke shared in his memoirs are of theatrical play, running around the city's northwest section with his cousins and friends, reading detective stories, going to entertainments, playing baseball—and enjoying the full attention and company of the numerous cousins, aunts, and uncles that made up the Kennedy and Ellington families. Edward was not recognized as an outstanding student or a musical prodigy. He was more interested in baseball at the time and did not practice enough even to perform solo in a recital—he played the bass part, while his teacher played the right hand notes he had failed to learn. But music lessons at that time were very comprehensive—even theory was taught in school; so Ellington may have absorbed more knowledge and training than he admitted in his later accounts of having more or less stumbled into this career. But it was the ragtime and stride piano players that he heard on the Washington entertainment circuit that caught his ear. Hearing James P. Johnson and his "Carolina Shout," he knew this was music he wanted to play, and he applied himself with diligence to imitate this new and exciting music. He was only fourteen, working one summer at the Poodle Dog Café, when he wrote his own "Soda Fountain Rag."

Among Ellington's school buddies was Jerome Rhea, "Jerry" to his friends. Duke would often go to the Rhea home for lunch or stop by after school. Annetta Rhea Smith, Jerry's sister, was only six years younger than Duke. Shortly before her ninety-fourth birthday, she recalled their long association. "Duke was in and out of the house like children are. They'd come in . . . my mother would make a sandwich for 'em—and then he'd go play the piano until she'd get tired of it. She'd say, 'That's long enough at that piano. Go out and play.'"³

Duke's own account of his adolescence suggests he was an enterprising young man. He hawked hot dogs at Griffith Stadium, where the Washington Senators played. He worked as a soda-jerk at the Poodle Dog Café and as a messenger for the War and Navy Department in 1917 and 1918. He played hooky from school, and part of his education, musical and otherwise, came from hanging around the local pool halls, which were frequented by men of all classes and professions, including musicians. He and his friends also somehow managed to check out the burlesque shows and other entertainment venues that his mother would not have sanctioned. When the adolescent Duke discovered that playing the piano also made him a hit at parties and the object of female attention, he had added incentives to develop these skills. His friend Edna Thompson, also a talented player, had lived near Duke during much of their youth. While he was a student at Armstrong Technical High School, she went to Dunbar High, a model of black education, where the music instructors had advanced degrees and were also performers.

Once Duke had acquired enough skill to play at parties and dances, there were plenty of opportunities for paying gigs. He soon learned that he could make more money by acting as his own publicist and booking agent. He also made friendships with other musicians and could provide a small band if needed. Arthur Whetsol, trumpet; and Otto Hardwick, bass and saxophone, were key players in Ellington's first group, called "the Duke's Serenaders." By the time he was a senior in high school, his income was quite good from the combination of painting signs and playing for everything from wealthy society parties in Virginia to dances at the True Reformers' Hall in Washington. He and his friends also appeared at Murray's Casino and Louis Thomas's cabaret. Duke became acquainted with banjoist Elmer Snowden

The Development of Jazz

When jazz emerged as an identifiable form of music, roughly in the second decade of the twentieth century, keepers of the cultivated musical tradition denounced it as a threat to decency. Jazz was associated with Storyville in New Orleans, the only legal red-light district in the country. The houses of ill repute all had their piano players, and such was the setting for Jelly Roll Morton's rise to fame. Probably of Creole origin, the word jazz, or *jass*, as it was first spelled, is a vulgarity denoting the sexual act. Jazz music was "hot"; it stirred the blood, prompted the body to respond to its rhythms, and provoked strong emotional responses for both performer and listener alike.

The Jazz Age of the 1920s ushered in a revolution in social mores, from Victorian propriety and values associated with duty and self-control to self-expression, sexual freedom, hedonism, and decadence. Under Prohibition ordinary citizens became lawbreakers and a huge illegal industry controlled by gangsters came into being. In spite of these associations, however, the elements of jazz had origins that predate its performance in night-life settings, whether a cheap brothel or an elegant nightclub. Duke Ellington used to say that jazz may have been played in brothels, but it didn't start there.

The rhythms, sounds, musical forms, and preferred instruments of early jazz are linked to sacred origins, through the black church and through an African tradition in which all music was understood as holy. Early in this nation's history there were slave festivals that allowed the preservation of stories, songs, and dance from the African traditions. Later on, drumming was outlawed because it was a highly refined system of communication.

However, in New Orleans' Congo Square drumming and dancing were allowed, and there was a mingling of Creole and Caribbean influences. The vocal tradition included the call-and-response pattern, scales with flatted thirds and fifths. There were vocal slides and bent notes (where the pitch is altered by semitones), glissandos, shouts, hollers, and melismas. These vocal expressions of pain and hope were later imitated by the players of reed and brass instruments in jazz ensembles. There were cultural crossovers, too, between these black musical creations and traditional hymns and folk music. Another influence was the rousing sound of marching bands that proliferated after the Civil War. Jazz ensembles typically included the cornet, clarinet, tuba, trombone, drums, and banjo—all of which could be played while marching. Later, the saxophone, stand-up bass, and piano were employed.

One of fourteen
different Ellington
family residences.
Duke lived here as a
teenager. (Courtesy
Ruth Ellington
Collection, Archives
Center, NMAH)

**Duke with a group of friends at Louis Thomas's cabaret circa
1920.** (Courtesy Dance Collection, Yale Music Library)

Daisy Kennedy Ellington, about age 30. (Courtesy Dance Collection, Yale Music Library)

and drummer Sonny Greer, who filled the heads of Duke and his friends with tales about the great music scene in New York City.

Duke had been listening and learning all he could from local piano players such as Oliver "Doc" Perry, Louis Brown, and Louis Thomas, all trained musicians; but it was Henry Lee Grant who offered to teach Duke harmony at his home twice a week. Grant, a composer and pianist, was one of several teachers on the Dunbar High music faculty. He was involved in a host of professional music activities.

In spite of his interest in music, it was Duke's artistic talent that won him a scholarship to attend Pratt Institute of Applied Arts in Brooklyn. Ellington turned it down and left high school before he graduated. He and Edna Thompson were married in July 1918 and moved into their own home at 1955 Third Street NW. Their son Mercer was born the following year. A second child died in infancy, probably sometime in 1920. Duke had registered for the draft, but was never called.

Was Edward Kennedy Ellington destined to become a composer and musician? These very early choices may have determined this direction. He clearly had a talent for both drawing and painting as well as music. In fact, on both sides of his family there was artistic talent in both music and visual art. J.E. and Daisy were musical, and cousins, too, demonstrated various artistic talents. But the life of a painter is unlike that of a musician, especially for a talented African American in the early part of the twentieth century. For one thing, the financial rewards of an artist's career were very unpredictable; whereas the demand for musical entertainment was high. Duke was enterprising and seemed to have been very ambitious from a young age. He was also stimulated by the enormous revolution going on in music at the time. It was ragtime that prompted him to try the piano again after stopping lessons. When he first began performing, he was playing the dance music of the times—fox-trots and waltzes, two-step. But he had an artist's ability to perceive and absorb elements of his environment, whether visual or aural. His bearing and style endeared him to others; and his young life, in spite of any hardships endemic to the times, was an experience of hospitality, community, and celebration of life.

A public career that would include these elements suited him, even though another aspect of his personality craved mental isolation and emotional privacy. The sensitivity that later helped him to recognize and bring out the peculiar talents of his musical colleagues may have been there even in his youth. Thus Ellington's creative instincts found expression in musical form and pitch instead of line and color. "If he had maybe the kind of thing that could have been abstract expressionism in painting, he could have gone on there," said Ulanov. "But he needed to have the kind of freedom— not just improvisation—it's the freedom not to have to isolate a specific content, which music is."

Ellington also lived in a time when certain avenues were open to black musicians; practically speaking, it was a good choice. When he began, perhaps he was pursuing money and social approval and the enjoyment of music itself, just following his natural desires. But he was caught up in the tide of a new music that would become prototypical of twentieth-century life in the United States and ended up shaping that music in profound and lasting ways. The combination of desire and opportunity was synergistic: elements of jazz were incorporated into his early compositions and performances; he, in turn, indelibly influenced the development of jazz and eventually revealed and enhanced its character as art. He wanted to be a "great musician," but could he have imagined what that greatness would entail—or cost?

Duke recorded "Black Beauty" as a solo piano piece in 1928. (Courtesy Duke Ellington Collection, Archives Center, NMAH)

The famous Cotton Club Orchestra. (Courtesy Dance Collection, Yale Music Library)

4

Harlem and Hollywood

What hath night to do with sleep?
—*John Milton*

THE COTTON CLUB WAS advertised as "the aristocrat of Harlem." Elaborate floor shows featured beautiful "high yaller" female dancers kicking, shaking, and shimmying in their scanty costumes with a choreographed grace that combined art and eroticism. Dancing couples, male tappers, and comedy routines added variety. The musical revues, with exotic African or languid Southern settings, showcased top-notch songs—written by Jimmy McHugh and Dorothy Fields. All entertainers were black, described in adjectives such as "Nubian" and "sepia," as well as the standard polite term "colored." But only white patrons dressed in their most elegant finery were admitted to view what critics called "sizzling, scorching entertainment."

Such a venue required a house dance band of high quality, an orchestra of ten or more pieces that could produce a variety of music for the floor shows and for dancing by the customers. Of course, the band, too, had to be all-black to suit the implicit attraction of the club, which traded on an in-vogue fascination with Africa and attributed a primitive physicality to people of color.

Both King Oliver and Fletcher Henderson, whose bands had greater experience and reputation than The Washingtonians, turned down offers to occupy that bandstand in 1927. Jimmy McHugh, who was ready to open a new revue late that year, liked the sound of an up-and-coming group headed by Duke Ellington. So this band was suggested. In Duke's version of the story, he had to scramble to find enough players and, consequently, arrived hours late for an audition. But, as it turned out, the person in charge of hiring was also late that day. He missed the other auditions and gave Duke's group the job. According to other accounts, Duke's band was chosen and hired, but the band had a contract for an engagement in Philadelphia that ran into the first week of the Cotton Club's opening show. The word came down from gangsters in power that Duke's services were needed back in New York and he should be released from his contract. "Be big," the Philadelphia club owner was advised. "Be big or be dead." He decided to release the band from its contract, and The Duke Ellington Orchestra opened at the Cotton Club on December 4, 1927. The need to compose and perform "jungle music"—a term imposed on the orchestra by Cotton Club ethos—was a constriction of Ellington's talents, one that he lived with while subversively writing great music anyway. The Cotton Club shows were broadcast live on national radio, and by the time Duke ended that first engagement there, his band was famous both here and abroad.

Although it proved to be the turning point in Ellington's early career, the Cotton Club job wasn't the first break for Duke, Greer, Whetsol, Hardwick, and Snowden since they had returned to the city in 1923 after an unsuccessful foray in 1921. Thomas "Fats" Waller, whom they had met in Washington when he was accompanying a traveling burlesque show, had set them up for a job that didn't pan out. A singer named Ada "Bricktop" Smith, whom they had met in D.C., came to their rescue and got them a job at a class establishment called Barron's. They moved downtown near the theatre district to Forty-ninth Street and Broadway, a smoky basement club known as the Hollywood. The atmosphere wasn't great, but the location represented a big step in advancing their common fortunes. They were ready, but a little nervous, and on opening night Duke froze. His face was blank, his mind was blank. The band played on. His hands roamed aimlessly over the keys, but few notes were struck. Fortunately, this lapse was unnoticed or simply forgiven.

The Hollywood became the Club Kentucky (also called the Kentucky Club), and it was The Washingtonians' regular gig for about four years. During that time the band rehearsed Ellington's arrangements until they could play without music, and their close harmonies made them sound bigger than they were. Sonny Greer, the irrepressible and entertaining drummer, doubled as lookout for undercover agents enforcing Prohibition. He also did some vocals, but the band generally avoided the clowning around such groups were expected to add to their performance. The guys were all sharp dressers and easy to be with. Duke himself had a style and presence that made a lasting impression, and his arranging and piano playing grew increasingly sophisticated. To the heavy bass punctuation of stride and the syncopations of ragtime, he added ideas borrowed from one of his mentors, Willie "the Lion" Smith, who used to let Duke take his place at the piano and pocket tips during some early lean periods.

By the time The Washingtonians were playing at the Kentucky Club, they were well known among Harlem musicians. With increased exposure, their shows attracted an early morning crowd of show business people and other celebrities. There was Al Jolson and a chorus girl named Lucille LeSueur (Joan Crawford); also Jack Johnson, a black boxer who was world heavyweight champion until racial antagonism forced him out of the business. Members of the Paul Whiteman Orchestra would stop by after their show, and their leader would plop down a $50 or $100 tip on Duke's piano as a sign of his appreciation.

During these years Ellington's role in the band changed, too. Banjoist Elmer Snowden, who had been the manager and leader, left precipitously when the others suspected him of pocketing more than his share of their pay at Barron's. Ellington already had a strong role in the group, because he was writing arrangements and leading rehearsals. After Snowden's departure Duke handled more of the business dealings. However, many decisions were made by a consensus of the members, who were tied together by their history and a strong sense of group identity. The long stint at the Kentucky Club gave Ellington an opportunity to hone his arranging skills and build on the band's strengths. Duke wrote music for a revue called *Chocolate Kiddies*, which toured Europe for two years. Will Marion Cook, a black classical violinist, became his informal tutor in music theory and composition. Cook had an impressive career composing and conducting, and in 1898 his all-black revue *Clorindy* opened at a major house on Broadway. According to Ellington, Cook knew Duke wouldn't study at a conservatory. So he advised this young man to find the logical way to develop a melody or voice a chord, then go around it and let his "inner self" break through.

Another influence on Duke's developing style came from new members of the band. Charlie Irvis was a trombone player who took his place on the stand and proceeded to add what came to be called "jungle-istic" effects to the music. Using some household object as a mute on the bell of his horn, Irvis would growl and grunt, slide suggestively, shiver his tone like a saxophonist. Irvis hung around with two other players who were given to similar stylistic touches, trumpeter James "Bubber" Miley and fellow trombonist Joe Nanton. When Arthur Whetsol decided to return home, Miley was recruited to replace him. Nanton, who was dubbed "Tricky Sam" by Otto Hardwick, took over Irvis's place when Charley decided to play elsewhere. All three players contributed to the evolving style of The Washingtonians, and they were the catalysts for an approach that Duke would use the rest of his life. He used his players' individual talents and limitations, their musical idiosyncrasies and personal styles as sources of musical ideas and new tone colors for his compositional palette.

From Bubber Miley, especially, Duke learned the importance of paying attention to what was around him. Bubber showed him a way of translating sights into sound. The trumpet player would take his inspiration from an advertising sign, a name, an overheard phrase. He'd say the syllables slowly. He'd play around with pitch, inflection, and phrasing. Then Bubber would take up his horn and translate these sounds into riffs that imitated the rise and fall and cadence of the human voice. Another technique was to take a melodic line from a hymn in church, turn it on its head, convert a major interval to minor, vary the rhythm. Now he had a new jazz figure. What is more, Ellington was learning a meditative process essential to art. The meditative element of artistic creation comes from attending to and selecting something from the environment and submitting it to an interior process, through which the selected material becomes reinterpreted and transformed. In an artistic creation this reinterpretation—through the medium of a poem, a painting, a musical composition, a dance, or whatever—has the power to prompt recognition and a new awareness in others.

Irvis and Miley were from a rougher school, musically and otherwise, than The Washingtonians, and their gut-bucket growling changed the band's sound, which at first was often soft and sweet. Now an amalgam of many different elements was woven into their music, even in their versions of the tunes of the day, such as W.C.

Handy's "St. Louis Blues." The band was growing larger, too. On some nights the original five might be joined by up to three additional players. Hard drinking and all-night music-making became their way of life. The guys slept during the day, if at all, and rehearsed in the late afternoons or early evening. They thrived on the excitement of making their music. Harlem in those days was, Sonny Greer was to recall later, like heaven, like "going to Church." Everybody loved everybody, he said.[1] The "new Negro" had declared a moratorium on fear. People thronged in and out of each other's homes for rent parties with music and cheap booze. Those who could afford more frequented the cabarets and nightclubs. For Duke it must have been something like a grown-up version of his adolescence, when he hung out at the pool halls and entertainment venues, learning his street smarts by listening to what went on, rubbing shoulders with people from all walks of life. But now he was playing the music that made them dance, laugh, and applaud.

Edna had joined Duke in New York, and young Mercer was left to the care of grandparents except for the summer months. Mercer recalled that about the year 1924 they were all living in one room of Leonard Harper's house at 2067 Seventh Avenue. Harper was associated with Connie's Inn and the Kentucky Club. There was a bed and a couch in the room, and also a battery-operated radio and a wind-up Victrola. The house had no electricity. Young Mercer listened to records of marching bands, as well as his father's earliest recordings. His mother and father both lived the night life. The boy would wake up early and take the money left him to go get his breakfast at a place around the corner and up the street. Sometimes he'd have to fight local bullies laying for him and that quarter in his pocket.

Those years were hard on the child and hard on his parents' relationship. Back in Washington Duke and Edna had their own house, friends in common, and family nearby, the unifying constraints of common associations. Duke had the sympathetic ear of his mother, whom he counted on for advice. When they started out married life, Edna had a role in encouraging and supporting her husband's dual careers, and she received Duke's adoring attention. Years after their separation she recalled with some embarrassment the beautiful, loving sketches he made of her and Mercer, madonna-like portraits of her holding or nursing the infant boy. Duke was also fond of his baby sister Ruth, who was only three years older than Mercer. "I remember when I was four or five," Ruth said, "he'd come home—he was such a big, tall man—and pick me up and hug me so hard I would run under the table and hide." From Mercer's accounts, he didn't receive that kind of affection from his father in his early years.

Duke was charming and very attractive to women. Like his father, he would indulge in courtly and flowery compliments, such as "Gee, you make that dress look pretty." And when a lovely woman walked his way, his face would light up and his smile beam, not unlike a smitten schoolboy. Edna was jealous, and probably with good reason. Mercer later wrote that Duke was involved in an affair that precipitated a terrible fight between his mother and father. Duke ended up with a long cut that left a scar on his cheek. In later years, Ellington offered obviously fabricated stories about its origins—ending with reference to something "more personal" or to a "jealous woman." He developed a permanent distaste for conflict of any kind and usually kept a tight reign on his own temper. His way of showing disapproval was to ignore the offending person.

It was around 1929 or 1930 that Edna and Duke separated for good, although they never legally dissolved their marriage. Mercer came to New York to find his father living with another woman at a new address. Mildred Dixon, a dancer in a Cotton Club duo, was Duke's new love. About the same time, Duke arranged for his mother, father, and sister to join him in New York. Although J.E. at first resisted—he protested that he was capable of supporting his family—eventually all of them, with Duke and Mildred, were settled in a large apartment at 381 Edgecomb Avenue.

So while Ellington and his Washingtonians were engrossed in the music and the excitement of New York night life, there were also major changes in Duke's personal life. Around these—his separation, the loss of their second child—he kept a guarded privacy. He also cultivated a certain interior isolation and developed the ability to concentrate intensely on his musical ideas and personal reflections. These made it possible for him to compose and to think, no matter what else was going on around him. On stage, he would be all smiles and happily puckered eyebrows. His dramatic conducting techniques and carefully practiced flourishes at the piano were executed as much for visual effect as for evoking any particular sound. But then, in a moment sometimes caught by the camera, his face would reveal a somber mood, a poignant sadness. His life-celebrating music may have been, in Albert Murray's phrase, his way of "stomping the blues."

Even in those early years Duke was writing poetry and reading voraciously, especially books on black history and—always—the Bible. He read all the books through several times in his early twenties. He used to say that he had three educations: one from school, one at the pool hall, and one from the Bible. Without the latter, he said, you can't understand what you learned from the other two places. He had to carve out the time for this, train himself to total concentration when there were people and noise and distraction all around. But the conclusions of such activity were kept to himself; and his most honest and revealing public statements were disguised, spoken through trombone, saxes, drums,

An Early Ellington Masterpiece

"Black and Tan Fantasy" was created by the growl trumpet player Bubber Miley and Ellington. According to Ulanov, Miley said he based his somber opening theme and repeated improvisations on a spiritual called "Hosanna," which his mother used to sing. Another writer has said that the tune was suggested to Miley by his mother's constant humming of "The Holy City."[2] This piece, widely sung in white churches, was written by Stephen Adams and published in 1892.

The time structure of "The Holy City" chorus is easily heard as a subtext in "Black and Tan Fantasy," but the melody based on that refrain is introduced in a minor mode, giving it a bluesy character. The piece builds with succeeding choruses to a concluding phrase from a Chopin sonata, popularly known as the "Funeral March."[3] In "Black and Tan Fantasy" Ellington gathered the diverse elements of sacred music, the blues, plunger-mute tones of early jazz players, and a phrase from a European Romantic composer and organized them in a unique way. The piece is also an early example of Ellington's penchant for blurring distinctions between (or reversing definitions of) the sacred and the secular.[4] The term "black and tan" was coined to describe black nightclubs that welcomed whites along with their regular clientele. The title of this composition, consequently, sug-

gests the flouting of convention, but the music, echoing the dark tones of hymns and mournful dirges, evokes the atmosphere of an old wayside chapel. One can almost smell the dusty plank floor and plain uncushioned pews.

This same juxtapostion was emphasized at a "trumpet duel" between Miley and Johnny Dunn at the Lafayette Theatre sometime in the 1920s, according to an unconfirmed story. First Dunn appeared, resplendent in a white tuxedo and played his best strutting stuff. When time came for Bubber to play, he did not step out on the stage, front and center. Instead, the stage curtain opened to reveal a country church setting. Duke was playing in the background while a series of wails was heard offstage. When Miley did appear, he was dressed as a preacher. His sermon, of course, was "Black and Tan Fantasy," and Bubber's message was so convicting that Johnny Dunn could not bear to stay and hear the end of it.

Ellington's classic piece figures in the 1929 RKO film *Black and Tan*. In this movie short Ellington's music linked two different worlds: the nightclub and the black church (represented by the presence of The Hall Johnson singers). Ellington, his trumpet player Arthur Whetsol, and actress Fredi Washington play characters much like themselves in their professional lives. In the opening scene in Duke's studio apartment, he is at his piano coaching Arthur Whetsol on his new composition. (Bubber Miley had only recently left the orchestra.) Fredi enters to tell Duke she has landed jobs for them in a club, she as a dancer and he as piano player. Duke reminds her of doctor's orders to give up her dancing, but she waves aside his objections. The locale shifts to the unnamed club, where black male tap-dancers in tuxedos perform in close-order drill across a mirrored floor to the accompaniment of Ellington's orchestra. Backstage, Fredi is so ill that she sees the dancers and the band in a kaleidoscopic mirage, an effective film technique. But she makes her solo entrance on cue and begins a frenzied dance to "Cotton Club Stomp." The beaded strands of her revealing costume fly around her as she twirls faster and faster until she finally collapses. As she is carried offstage, Duke is ordered to keep on playing, and the female dancers in feathered costumes (actual Cotton Club performers) begin a shimmying routine. A stagehand sent to get Duke is intercepted by the manager. Duke then responds, without hesitation, telling the band to pack up and storming off the stage.

In a highly stylized deathbed scene, Fredi's room is filled with members of the orchestra and the members of the Hall Johnson Choir, whose voices are heard first singing the words "Same train carried my mother." The heightened shadows of players and singers are projected on a far wall. With Ellington at her side, Fredi says, "Duke, play me the 'Black and Tan Fantasy.'" Both the choir and the orchestra begin the theme at a slow tempo. The choir continues to sing, seeming to intone the sound of church bells or a repeated two-word phrase that is indiscernible. Then instrumental soloists enter, with growls, whinnies, and high-pitched wails that build in intensity to a point where the choir comes back in. As the beautiful dancer breathes her last, the music reaches its concluding "Funeral March" line. But the singing voices continue, waning through a coda that sounds unresolved. In the last frame Duke's face is blurred out of focus, his eyes brimming with tears.[5]

bass, trumpets—and piano. In some of his earliest pieces there is a thread of melancholy, a hint of longing that colors what appears, at first hearing, to be a rough and rollicking, even humorous, invitation to dance. It can be heard in "Black Beauty," a piece dedicated to the Cotton Club dancer Florence Mills and recorded as a piano solo by Ellington. "Black and Tan Fantasy" (also spelled "Fantasie") is another piece that has an underlying spiritual quality, despite the quirky effects employed.

Ellington had begun publishing his music and recording it, too, during the years 1924 to 1926. The two enterprises were ideally linked. When a new recording was heard, people wanted to buy the music and play it themselves. If they bought the music first, then they wanted to hear the recording. To take advantage of yet another avenue to popularity and commercial success, Duke needed to align himself with someone associated with Tin Pan Alley, the district where sheet-music publishing, recording, and band bookings were headquartered. Initially the band worked with an agent who arranged its summer tours to New England dance halls and clubs in 1926 and 1927. That's when Duke met Johnny Hodges and Harry Carney, two young reed players. For a brief time, the famed New Orleans clarinetist Sidney Bechet played with Ellington in New York.

Meanwhile, Ellington's path had crossed that of Irving Mills, a young man working with his older brother in the music business. It's not unlikely that Duke may have tried to sell some tunes to Irving or to Jack Mills, his brother. The Washingtonians had recorded some blues and popular songs; also a few original compositions, for minor labels. Some were not even released. But Mills could offer The Washingtonians more opportunities to record, and he was an enterprising and well-connected businessman. Mills later identified "Black and Tan Fantasy" as the piece that "bowled him over" when he heard The Washingtonians at the Kentucky Club sometime in 1926. He knew, even then, that in Duke Ellington he had encountered a great American artist.[6] Shortly after that, Mills approached Ellington about a business arrangement. The terms of their first agreement are not known, but later Duke and Irving each received forty-five percent of an unusual and mutually beneficial partnership; the remainder went to their attorney. The business alliance they formed dramatically changed their lives, and those of the men in the band as well, who now had become employees in a venture headed by Ellington and Irving.

Ellington's partnership with Mills brought the band new opportunities, but forever changed its character in some significant ways. Mills was not simply a business partner. Mills wrote some lyrics, and he was better at this than Duke was. But his name also went on many pieces as a co-composer, a practice that probably had to do more with division of royalties than with artistic collaboration. Mills also had a good sense of what the public would accept, how far out on a limb Duke could go without losing his audience or market. But in spite of the commercial angle that Mills was attuned to, he did recognize Ellington's superior talent and had the vision to present him as a unique American musical artist and composer, rather than simply as a bandleader. A short film of Mills introducing bands in the 1930s makes this clear. Barron Lee's Blue Ribbon Band is described as one that plays sweet or "hot jazz," with "echoes of the jungle, weird and barbaric." Mills introduces Duke Ellington as "one who seems to be set entirely apart from all other composers and musicians. . . . Today he is acclaimed by music authorities both here and abroad as the creator of a new vogue in music."

The Ellington ensemble by the late 1920s had expanded to sometimes seven, eight, or nine players, including Tricky Sam Nanton, Miley, Hardwick, Ellington, Freddy Guy, Greer, and Henry

"Bass" Edwards on tuba. In 1927 Harry Carney, only seventeen years of age, replaced Otto Hardwick, whose temporary leave turned into three years. Carney developed a special sound on the baritone sax that anchored the band for almost fifty years. Then alto saxophonist Johnny Hodges came on board. He, too, except for a relatively short departure during the 1950s, spent his life with Duke as one of jazz's outstanding soloists. Nanton and Greer also stayed with the band for decades. Small ensembles from the larger orchestra made records under names such as the Hotsy Totsy Gang, the Jungle Band, the Six Jolly Jesters, the Harlem Foot-warmers, Mills' Ten Blackberries, Sonny Greer and His Memphis Men. This practice allowed them to record for different companies, but it also reflected Ellington's attention to small groups and to the need for his players to express their individual styles of leadership.

Mills delivered on his promise to record the band. There were good contracts, and lots of extra work, too. The 78 rpm records could accommodate about three minutes of music on each side, and this became a defining limit for writing popular music. Then Ellington wrote and recorded "Creole Rhapsody, Parts I and II," developing its musical themes into a six-minute composition. Whether it was the unique gifts of his sidemen or the mechanical apparatus of the recording studio, the environment around him was raw material for Ellington's expanding art.

Ellington's work at the Cotton Club stretched his compositional skills, too. The variety of acts required him to come up with new numbers that were worked out in collaboration with the performers. The venue functioned as another kind of conservatory for him, and some of his greatest music was produced during his first engagement there. (Ellington returned for an extended appearance in 1937, after the Club was moved downtown to Broadway in the aftermath of a Harlem riot.) It was during this time that Ellington produced "Echoes of the Jungle,"

"Jubilee Stomp," "The Mooche," "Awful Sad," "Black Beauty," "Creole Love Call," "Stompy Jones," and "Rockin' in Rhythm." "Shout 'Em, Aunt Tillie" evoked the spirit of revival meetings.

Besides "Black and Tan Fantasy," the band's theme song stands out among Ellington's early compositions. "East St. Louis Toodle-O" was also written by Ellington and Miley. "Mood Indigo" was recorded in 1930. The piece was remarkable not only for its smooth chromaticism and dream-like feeling. Ellington's genius was further demonstrated in the unusual chord voicings given to the clarinet, trombone, and trumpet playing the opening "A" section. On the "B" section or bridge, whoever took the solo was free to embellish and improvise. Russell Procope, who in later years was the featured clarinet soloist on the number, must have played it thousands of times, but each performance was a little different in phrasing or melodic embellishments. Procope said that he never grew tired of it.

The confidence of Irving Mills in Duke's professional abilities proved to be well-founded, and Mills delivered the opportunities that kept the band before the public. After making the remarkable short feature *Black and Tan* in 1929, the orchestra traveled to Hollywood in 1930. The occasion was their appearance in the full-length feature movie *Check and Double Check*, a lightweight effort to capitalize on the popularity of the radio show *Amos and Andy*, played by two white comedians mimicking blacks. For that appearance Barney Bigard, a Creole, and Puerto Rican Juan Tizol were required to black their faces. However, compared to the degrading depictions of other African Americans in the film, Ellington and his orchestra looked both smart and accomplished as they played several of their original tunes in white high-society ballroom scenes.

In the Wall Street crash of 1929, Duke had taken some personal losses, but he never was out of work. The Great Depression had begun to take its toll on the country, and the reckless abandon of the 1920s had given way to despair. Among those who suffered most from the country's economic woes were African Americans. The golden days of Harlem were fading fast. What would happen to the music that was so much a part of the short-lived prosperity and superficial glamour of the Jazz Age? Ellington left the Cotton Club early in 1931. He had gained enough recognition for Mills to arrange successful appearances in major theatres across the country. His music was a tonic to a disheartened people, who could come to hear the live orchestra on stage in huge, ornately appointed movie theatres, then stay for a feature film. The trip included three different bookings in Chicago over the months-long tour. For the opening at the Oriental Theatre on Friday, February 13, Ellington hired Ivie Anderson as his first regular vocalist. She had to take four bows before a packed house of thirty-two hundred fans, and applause for the band went on and on. The show was a major sensation and an unqualified financial success. In one week, the theatre grossed nearly $50,000 on that first appearance, and in five later bookings that year, all previous house records were broken—for both profits and people. Cumulatively about four-hundred thousand people attended these performances.

Despite these triumphs, Duke had to deal with frustrations that thwarted his personal desire for peace and escape from conflict. The band had to find housing in private homes of fellow African Americans. Duke on occasion might be allowed to stay in a fine hotel, but his musicians would have been turned away. They all had to be careful where they ate and, especially in the case of white women, with whom they were friendly. And there were always subtle reminders that a black man's best would never be good enough in a color-conscious society.

On that tour Duke was fined $2,000 by the autocratic James Petrillo, head of the musicians' union, for paying his band members pennies below the hourly wage scale in Chicago—an infraction that amounted to about $60 total. There are several stories about run-ins with Chicago small-time gangsters, attempted extortions—even a threatened kidnapping. Once Cotton Club owner Owney Madden was called on to use his underworld connections to get Duke out of a jam. Al Capone sent his ambassadors to negotiate an end to this bullying. The stories made good copy later. But when band members, carrying no metal but their instruments, were in the middle of armed factions, they weren't laughing.

Duke had been working almost a decade to realize his ambitions as a composer. Though he had reached a certain level of fame and even artistic success by the early 1930s, where could he go from there? There were still racial barriers, however much he refused to dwell on them. His fans were divided. Some just enjoyed the music for its own sake. Others saw art and transcendental meaning in his compositions. Whatever his own leanings and direction, he would be challenged to keep the favor of distinctive camps.

Reflecting on these years with *New Yorker* magazine writer Richard O. Boyer, Ellington recalled that the initial happiness of his Harlem club days had soon worn thin. He became tired of obnoxious drunks and boors. He called the music business "just another racket." Poor material became hit songs; publishers wanted him to write to their specifications. Failing to appreciate Ellington's continual experimentation, even ardent fans became an irritation when they complained that a piece didn't sound exactly as it did on last year's recording. The Duke grew moody and depressed. He was tempted to quit. His friends were worried about him, but it was his business partner who came up with a prescription that proved beneficial for both the man and his career.

In the early 1930s Duke Ellington and His Orchestra often appeared on stage with dancers such as "Snake Hips" Tucker. Ivie Anderson was the first full-time vocalist with the band. (Courtesy Dance Collection, Yale Music Library)

Early publicity shot for Duke's venture into Hollywood. (Courtesy Dance Collection, Yale Music Library)

The composer at work, late 1930s. (Courtesy Dance Collection, Yale Music Library)

5

Lost and Found

The true paradises are paradises we have lost.
—*Marcel Proust*

IRVING MILLS, PROMPTED BY the overseas popularity of the band's recordings and similar trips by Louis Armstrong and Cab Calloway, arranged a tour of England, Holland, and France. The year was 1933. Duke was plagued by worries, fears of crossing the Atlantic, and a vague feeling that he wasn't meant to be too happy. But after the liner made the trip safely and the group arrived by train in London, Ellington, Mills, the band, and other performers in the company were greeted by a large welcoming committee of photographers, a beginning that presaged the general tenor of the trip. The orchestra's visit had been well prepared for, and its leader and members were presented as artists of the first order. Hotel accommodations, however, remained something of a problem. One famous man who was "not very black" might be allowed, but not eighteen. The reigning jazz monarch was able to stay at the prestigious Dorchester. But less famous members of his court were dispersed over the city in rooming houses and lesser hotels.

Ellington's company opened at the Palladium with a smashing thirteen-act stage show. The BBC paid a record amount to broadcast the band. In addition, there were concert performances with elaborate programs that often didn't even mention the word "jazz." Other appearances in England were comparably successful, though not without incident. The *Melody Maker* sponsored two London concerts a few weeks apart. At the first one the audience laughed at Tricky Sam Nanton's trombone embellishments and generally responded to such uses of Ellington's instrumental tonal palette as bits of novel trickery. In response Duke played less innovative material in the second half of the program. This concession to popular tastes horrified his serious devotees. In the second concert program the eminent jazz writer Spike Hughes instructed the audience not to laugh at Nanton nor to applaud during numbers. In the press, some writers used words like "ugly" and "crude" in dismissing Ellington's innovations.

But others couldn't find enough superlatives. For composer Constant Lambert, hearing the Ellington brass section was the thrill of a lifetime. Others ranked Ellington's compositional genius with that of Bach and Debussy. Major composers–such as Percy Grainger in New York, Igor Stravinsky, Darius Milhaud–were generous with their praise. Ellington's "Creole Rhapsody" had already been awarded New York School of Music's prize as best composition of the year. And the writer R.D. Darrell wrote passionately of Ellington's art: No other composer—popular or serious—had gone as far as Ellington in exploiting tonal coloring. A British writer covering the tour said that Ellington's music possessed a universality comparable to Shakespeare's. In Paris the reception was equally warm. Three concerts were played at the huge Sale Pleyel. French musicians knew the recorded solos by heart and were full of questions for Ellington's sidemen. Though some of them were well-schooled, the Americans had never received such knowledgeable appreciation of their gifts in their homeland. They were overwhelmed by this kind of respect —from white people—for the craft they had learned in years of

listening and playing, of drawing from inside themselves meanings they did not often express in words.

On the long voyage back to the States, Duke had time to
ponder this experience. What it gave him was *spirit*, he later told
biographer Ulanov. The reception he and the band received had
lifted him out of a "bad groove." If these people thought he was
important, maybe he had said something after all. Maybe his
music did "mean something." After the orchestra's triumphant
tour of Europe, Mills arranged a swing through New England
and began talking up a southern tour, which would be highly
profitable. Duke wasn't interested in the South, for any amount
of money. But a solution was hit upon for avoiding, as much as
possible, the humiliation of southern inhospitality toward
blacks. Typically two railroad cars were secured for the band.
Another car carried instruments and stage equipment. Until the
1950s the band members traveled together in private railroad
cars, usually two Pullmans and dining car as well. Especially in
southern states, Ellington said, it was an arrangement that commanded respect: "We travel the way the President does."

The tour opened in Dallas at the Majestic Theatre, originally
a vaudeville stage, with twenty-four hundred seats and a Roman
garden decorative theme. Carole Lombard starring in the movie
Brief Moment shared the marquee billing. Once again records for
attendance and gross revenues were broken by "Duke Ellington
and his Band." Moreover, local prejudices were subtly challenged
in the publicity for Duke's visit and in his quoted interviews by the
press, which demonstrated remarkable respect for Ellington's
achievements. His music kept both white and black couples spin-
ning on the floor—at separate, segregated dance-hall engagements.

While Ellington traveled, Daisy, J.E., Ruth, Mercer, and Mildred were living together at Edgecomb Avenue. This Harlem

"Sugar Hill" address and a new Pierce-Arrow automobile for his mother and father were provided by the substantial income Ellington was making from records, sheet music, and touring appearances. Mercer described their prosperity as a kind of "culture shock" for him, compared to the family home in Washington. His nice clothes created animosities at the public schools he attended with children who were more affected by the ravages of those Depression years. When she was about fifty, Daisy had put J.E. "out of the bedroom," said Ruth, who was in high school at the time. Duke did not want Mercer or Ruth to attend private schools, but Ruth was enrolled in an all-girls public school. She later joked that she was "kept locked up in the bathroom" during those years. The family living arrangements paired Mercer with J.E. in one bedroom, Ruth and her mother in another, and Duke and Mildred in the master bedroom.

But Aunt Daisy, as they called her, was not well. While Duke was away Mildred expressed her concern and even arranged for her and Duke's own doctor to provide medical advice. But Daisy refused his recommendations for further examination and, eventually, hospitalization. In 1934, the same year Mercer finished junior high school, she returned to Washington for her own remedy, "massaging treatments." On the telephone with her son, she avoided questions about her health. That summer Duke was writing the music for the 1935 short film feature *Symphony in Black*. In September 1934 on Brunswick he recorded "Saddest Tale," which discographer Eddie Lambert has described as "one of the greatest blues ever written" and a "perfect work of art." In his recorded singing debut, Duke introduced the opening lines himself in a "croaking, halting, feverish voice."[1] This choked cry was a "reflection of his gloom" as he worried over his mother's deteriorating health, according to Lambert. The piece was later incorporated into a segment called

"Blues" in the film, but the words were changed to depict a woman's sadness when she's left by her man.

When Daisy finally checked into a highly respected Detroit hospital in 1935, it was too late to arrest the cancer. Duke arranged his schedule to be near her. For her last three days alive, he was at her bedside day and night, often with his head on her pillow. On May 27, surrounded by her family, Daisy Kennedy Ellington died. Duke had spent his thirty-sixth birthday expecting his mother to die and praying for her to live. Their relationship was marked by mutual devotion, financial support, and physical proximity. There was a psychological complexity, too, that had to affect all his other relationships with women detrimentally. It was his mother's approval and praise that Duke worked so hard for. It was her faith that had inspired his desires to be great; her ideal love that, once lost, could never be duplicated. He would always remain tied to her.

After her passing he struggled to regain his motivation for working. He was in a state of despair from which nothing seemed to lift him, not even the Scriptures he pored over. Brooding and melancholic, he withdrew into his own thoughts. Ruth was nineteen at the time her mother died. Duke felt a new responsibility for Ruth, who was a bright student majoring in biology at New College of Columbia University; but she also worried over him and assumed her mother's attitude of devotion. "I believe he came to see she was in God's hand's, and happy, and that he was to carry on," she said.

When Ellington was able to return to his music again, this experience of loss and melancholia became raw material for a new composition—the longest Ellington had written to that point. Called "Reminiscing in Tempo," it was a concert piece twelve minutes in length and required two sides of two records when it was recorded in September of 1935. Ellington described the work as beginning in a "soliloquizing mood," with pleasant thoughts. Then comes a downward pull, a sense of loss, followed finally by an affirmative ending. Even though a son's grief was the emotional impetus for this work, the result is not simply an outpouring of feeling. Some degree of observation and recollection of a process is necessary to shape a work of art. Even Ellington's description of "Reminiscing in Tempo" reveals that a trauma has led to new awareness which brings, if not tranquility, at least the acceptance of loss.

Ellington wrote the piece while traveling by train on tour again in the South, when he had the "mental isolation to reflect on the past." The rhythms and fading pitches created by the train and others passing by contribute to its general mood of nostalgia. In his memoirs Duke wrote that the musical statement was a "detailed account of my aloneness" after the loss of his mother. He was thus able to express something he "could never have found words for."[2] The piece is basically one theme with thirteen variations. It is characterized by complex harmonic structures and an interweaving of asymmetrical melodic motifs. This complexity, and the piece's dissimilarity to earlier and shorter works, baffled the critics and created a stir when the recording was released. Like many of Ellington's thrusts into new territory, the work was a marketing headache for the record company and a source of debate for fans and critics. Irving Mills later said the record should never have been released. He identified this work as the beginning of an unfortunate departure from Ellington's style.

John Hammond, an early fan of Ellington, was especially critical at the time the piece came out. Only Leonard Hibbs, writing in an English magazine, went beyond his initial impression to do a careful analysis of the music and discern patterns in the statement and restatements, the organization of instrumental solos. He concluded that Ellington had allowed his listeners to "'tune-in' on his mind at work."[3]

Sometime in 1936 Ellington became friends with a young man by the name of Edmund Anderson. Anderson's mother was a pianist, and they sometimes listened to broadcasts from the Cotton Club. When Anderson first heard Ellington's orchestra, he said, "This is extraordinary." He went out and bought all Duke's records. This was in the 1920s, but they didn't meet until much later. "We became great friends the very first night we met," said Anderson. "He would come down to my apartment and play the piano, and we'd talk, and I'd play records for him. He had been compared to Delius when he went to England, and I don't think he'd ever heard much Delius. And I played Delius and Ravel, Stravinsky, and even Edgar Varese, a modern composer who wrote one piece just for percussion instruments alone. We listened to lots of jazz, too. Those were wonderful days."[4]

Anderson was a stockbroker then, working for his father on Wall Street. He started taking off in the afternoon to go hear Ellington's recording sessions. "You ought to give a concert in Carnegie Hall," he told Duke and offered to produce it. At that time, there had been very few jazz concerts at Carnegie. Anderson had approval for Ellington and his orchestra to have their own concert on a date of their choosing. The only thing needed was for a date to be reserved on the band's schedule. Anderson said he kept calling Irving Mills to get a commitment, but never could. He blames Mills for the fact that Ellington did not make his Carnegie debut until several years later.

Anderson met the rest of Ellington's family including J.E., who had become closer to his son since Daisy's death. J.E. looked forward to his son's homecomings from his touring. Ellington's father lived intemperately. He loved his liquor and his tobacco and the company of pretty women. He developed a bad cough the autumn of 1937 after lending his coat to a "fair damsel," as the story goes.[5] "Uncle Ed" had to be taken to The Presbyterian Hospital at the Columbia University Medical Center, not far from the family quarters. Duke and Ruth were there near midnight on the October evening when James Edward Ellington died. It was Ruth, a year away from graduating college, who arranged for funeral services in New York and at the John Wesley A.M.E. Zion Church back in Washington, where J.E. was buried beside his wife's grave.

Duke had relapsed into despair again. The loss of his father precipitated another period of going through the routines of his demanding life without the spark of creativity and joy it characteristically brought to him. Another source of sadness was the loss of Arthur Whetsol, who had left the band because of a brain tumor. He was the veteran in the trumpet section, Duke's old friend from Washington days. Even after he stopped playing there were years of misery and mental disintegration before he died. Freddie Jenkins, another trumpet player, had left the band in 1934 because of tuberculosis, but he slowly fought his way back to health.

Later in his life, Ellington avoided talk of death and virtually refused to attend funerals. People close to him were not even aware that as a young husband and father he had lost a child. But through his music in "Saddest Tale" and, especially, "Hymn of Sorrow" he speaks as a man who knows grief intimately. Then, as the artist, he presents to his listeners a gift that suggests healing even through the evocation of that sense of loss.

During the mid-1930s a major change had been taking place in jazz. Ellington's 1932 tune "It Don't Mean a Thing (If It Ain't Got That Swing)" had popularized the term "swing." The word has multiple meanings. It describes a musical concept central to syncopation in jazz, an emphasis on the off-beats, beat two and

A Symphony of Grief

An early film featuring Ellington and the orchestra is the 1935 feature *Symphony in Black: A Rhapsody of Negro Life*. It was built entirely around Ellington's music, with wordless dramatic vignettes bringing to life the four musical sequences: "The Laborers," "A Triangle" (Dance, Jealousy, Blues), "Hymn of Sorrow," and "Harlem Rhythm." The short bears the stamp of Ellington's sensibilities about his people and his own role in creating art from their historical experience and their folk music. It also contains two pieces with a thread of mourning: "Saddest Tale" and "Hymn of Sorrow."

"Hymn of Sorrow," a beautiful piece of pure mourning conveyed especially in the trumpet's melody line, was created by Ellington for the film. Its importance to him is revealed in comments quoted in an article written by Edward Morrow in December that same year. The topic was George Gershwin's recently premiered *Porgy and Bess*, which Ellington declared was not a true depiction of Negro life nor written in the Negro musical idiom, though it might be grand music. Morrow asked Ellington if he would say that an honest Negro musical play would have to contain social criticism, and Ellington answered, "Absolutely." In the episode concerning the death of a baby, he said he put into the dirge "all the misery, sorrow and undertones of the conditions" associated with that death. In summary, he said this piece was true to the life of the people in a way that *Porgy and Bess* was not.[6]

"Hymn of Sorrow" is followed joltingly by an upbeat dance scene to Ellington's music, which concludes the film. Ellington said he thought "Hymn of Sorrow" should have been the film's conclusion, but was not for "commercial reasons." This odd sequencing is not the only thing that undercuts the potential power of the funeral segment. The strength of Ellington's evocative lament was also bled by extraordinarily depersonalized visuals. Although the camera moves through the congregation, focusing on (mostly male) tearful black faces and hands clasped in prayer, the viewer has no clue that a child is in a casket beneath the pulpit of a wild-haired preacher or that there are grieving parents in the congregation. This striking omission Krin Gabbard attributes to editing by studio executives who assumed white audiences would be uncomfortable with the full-fledged humanity of black parents grieving over the loss of a child. It is not surprising that nothing of the social conditions or circumstances of the child's death are suggested visually—even if these were in Ellington's mind when he composed the music.

four in 4/4, or a forward-driving elasticity in subdivisions of the beat. This quality is most identified with Louis Armstrong's trumpet playing. As a descriptive term, "swing" is a synonym for pizzazz, zest, stylish sophistication. Ellington used to say, "If your pulse is with my pulse, then we're swinging." The word "swing" eventually became the label for a style of big-band jazz, which by 1935 had become America's popular music. After the Wall Street crash of 1929 had ushered in the Great Depression, and Prohibition had ended in 1934, America had left "the Jazz Age" behind and entered "the Swing Era." The roots of swing were in early jazz, and bands like those of Fletcher Henderson, Don Redman, Count Basie, and Ellington had laid the ground-work. This period saw the rise of other groups such as those of Glen Gray, Bennie Moten, Jimmie Lunceford, Chick Webb. Paul Whiteman remained popular, as did Guy Lombardo, who were more in the realm of dance orchestras.

But it was Benny Goodman, combining classical virtuosity with jazz, who gained a following for swing among young white college students. The Goodman band and small ensembles were racially integrated, too, which helped bridge the gap, at least cul-turally, between "hot jazz" players and the new big band style. The bands proliferated in number during the years when the country needed some diversion while going through hard times. This music was accessible to any household with a radio, and when the bands came to town, some people managed to find the money for a night at the huge theatres or the ballrooms that dot-ted the country.

Fans of early jazz and its regional variations didn't necessar-ily embrace the new style, which some considered a lamentable development. With more white fans, white bands like those of Bob Crosby, Tommy and Jimmy Dorsey, and, later, Glenn Miller came to the forefront. But Fats Waller, Count Basie, Chick

A 1930s jam session launching Master and Varsity records.
(Courtesy Dance Collection, Yale Music Library)

Program from Duke's 1933 tour of England. (Courtesy of Earl Okin)

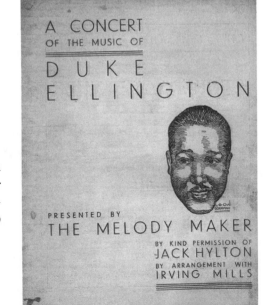

A CONCERT
OF THE MUSIC OF
D U K E
E L L I N G T O N

PRESENTED BY
THE MELODY MAKER
BY KIND PERMISSION OF
JACK HYLTON
BY ARRANGEMENT WITH
IRVING MILLS

The Maestro receives a new baton from his sister Ruth in 1943.
(Photographer: Bill Mork, Park Sheraton Hotel, New York City.
Courtesy Dance Collection, Yale Music Library)

**Three generations of Ellington men: Mercer, young Edward, and
Duke.** (Courtesy Dance Collection, Yale Music Library)

Webb, and Art Tatum headed black jazz orchestras identified with swing. Ellington's band was certainly popularly seen as being a leading interpreter of swing, but he never simply followed what was in vogue. He rode the wave while it was high, but still persisted in creating music that would survive when the tide moved out. Although the rhythmic vitality of his orchestra laid a foundation for other bands, swing as a category was simply too limiting for Ellington. He aspired to much, much more. However, The Benny Goodman Orchestra was featured when Carnegie Hall hosted an historic jazz concert on January 16, 1938. Count Basie also appeared. But Ellington declined to participate. He allowed some of his musicians to play in the bands on stage; but he sat in the audience—knowing his dream of premiering a major extended work was long overdue.

The person who was to become Ellington's single most significant musical collaborator came into his life during this period. Billy Strayhorn was a talented young musician from Pittsburgh. At a very young age he had written the music and lyrics of a song expressing the disillusion of a roué, a most challenging ballad called "Lush Life." He was an accomplished pianist but, as a black man, had little chance of a career performing the music of the Impressionistic composers he loved. He found that his homosexuality was an obstacle to his being accepted in black jazz bands. In Pittsburgh he was writing songs and playing jazz when he could, while dreaming of New York and Paris.[7]

In late 1938 Duke and the band were playing an engagement at Pittsburgh's Stanley Theatre. Billy was set up to meet Duke through the intercession of a friend and a man who knew the Negro band leaders well. Strayhorn got together some arrangements and compositions, and Ellington received him after a matinee performance. Duke asked Billy to play something for him. The young man, as short as Duke was tall, sat down and played "Sophisticated Lady" just as Ellington had performed it that day. Then Strayhorn played the piece in his own style. Duke called Harry Carney to hear this phenomenon. Over the next few days, Duke gave Billy several assignments and grilled him about his training and background. Finally he told Strayhorn he wanted to take him into the organization, possibly as a lyricist and arranger. He needed some time to figure it all out. Ellington wrote down directions on how to get to his Harlem apartment and instructed Billy to look him up.

But it was actually in Newark that Strayhorn caught up with him again, just when Duke was trying to get in touch with him. (He had lost Billy's phone number.) Billy presented him with a new song, one he had composed using Duke's directions for his inspiration. He titled it "Take the 'A' Train." Ellington hired him, without specifying either his duties or his pay. Strayhorn went back to Pittsburgh to pack, and Mercer was given the task of getting Billy set up at the YMCA once he got to New York City. Billy stayed there two nights. When Ellington returned from Europe, "Strays" was living with Ruth, Mercer, and Mildred like one of the family—and, with Mercer's help, he had become well acquainted with arrangements in the Ellington book.

Band members dubbed Strayhorn "Swee'pea," a nickname from the Popeye comic-strip. Baby-faced, shy, and polite, he was still confident in his own abilities. The rapport between the two men developed into a deep emotional bond. When it came to music, their communication seemed to approach telepathy. Together Duke and Strays formed an extraordinary creative partnership from which came some of Ellington's most sublime writing. "Strayhorn inspired Ellington with new ideas in melody, harmony, and orchestration," wrote Jeff Friedman, who teaches a course on Ellington's compositional style. "More than a collaborator in the usual sense of the word, Strayhorn became his full musical partner."[8] Ellington resisted efforts to characterize Strayhorn as his alter ego and typically called him his "writing and arranging companion."

In his memoirs Duke said that Billy was his right arm and his left arm, with "my brain waves in his head, and his in mine."[9] Strayhorn used to go to Barry Ulanov's apartment to listen to the classical music in his record collection. Ulanov observed the dynamics of their relationship while collecting material for his biography of Ellington. "I think that to some extent the relationship with Strayhorn was the second child of his life," he said. "Strayhorn had a difficult life as a homosexual in a world that wasn't open to that," said Ulanov. In his opinion, Billy's talent was the key. "Though Mercer was a good person and had some small talent, he was not in the same league with Strayhorn," said Ulanov. Billy "just had it" for Duke. He offered Billy a private attention and took pride in his work. And, added Ulanov, it was "paternal, not avuncular. He wasn't his uncle. He was his father. Duke's not denying Mercer for a moment; he's not disavowing Mercer. But Strayhorn was the connection. As a father of four myself I could just feel it, physically, in the way Duke responded to Strayhorn, and the way Strayhorn responded to Duke, when he presented his work to him. It was a son's offering, and very, very moving."

As Ellington moved into the 1940s, he had lost both his parents, and now he had more responsibility for the welfare of his sister Ruth, as well as for Mercer. Billy Strayhorn had entered his life and was to become a key relationship, whether as a second child or a beloved friend, as well as his most trusted critic and collaborator. At the same time, Duke was ending two key relationships, one personal and one professional. His domestic life with Mildred Dixon was coming to a close, and his business partnership with Irving Mills was to be dissolved. "Mildred Dixon was introduced to me as Mrs. Ellington," said Edmund Anderson. "And she was not. Duke used to call her 'Sweet Bebe.' Duke met Evie. That was the end of Mildred as far as he was concerned. Although he stayed friends with everybody—I mean, almost everybody—except maybe Evie. They lived together." The new woman in Ellington's life was Beatrice "Evie" Ellis, a Cotton Club showgirl whom he had fallen in love with when he played a return engagement at the relocated Cotton Club.

The break with Mills was initiated shortly before he was to leave on his second European tour. Theirs had been an immensely successful arrangement in many ways, and both men in later years described their parting as amicable. Some of their differences were over the direction of Ellington's musical explorations. But certainly by this time Ellington must have questioned an arrangement that put half his earnings into someone else's pockets. He had even been called a "musical sharecropper" by Adam Clayton Powell, Jr., a prominent Harlem clergyman. There was also criticism from the black press because Ellington had not employed any black lyricists.

Ellington's strong feelings for his mother may also have played a role in this break with Irving Mills. According to Anderson, Mills failed to comply with Ellington's request to obtain an expensive casket for his mother's burial. Another story is that Duke walked into the Mills office one day and asked to look at the books. A short time later he initiated the break. Whatever the actual circumstances, Ellington and Mills came to an agreement about division of rights and properties. Duke secured the services of the William A. Morris booking agency and a new music publisher.

Mills had already arranged a second European tour during 1939, and that was to include Sweden, Denmark, Norway, Holland, and Belgium. The shadow of the Nazi swastika was already hanging over Europe, and evidence of the looming war was everywhere. The band found a train ride through Germany ominously troubling. In spite of that, this European tour was another great tonic for Ellington, who celebrated his fortieth birthday royally in Stockholm that year.

"Take the 'A' Train" by Billy Strayhorn became the band's theme song in the early 1940s. (Courtesy Duke Ellington Collection, Archives Center, NMAH)

6

Dreams and Realities

My soul has grown deep like the rivers.

—Langston Hughes

THE DECADE OF THE 1940s brought Ellington opportunities to hatch some dreams that had long been incubating—even as it ushered in some lean years for Ellington's orchestra and decimated the country's big bands as the United States moved into post-World War II cultural shifts. Ellington had signed with RCA Victor as part of his mid-life career moves, and its recording studios and personnel provided a supportive environment for Ellington's dedicated work for several years. Strayhorn's gifts began to come to the fore and opened up previously unexplored paths for Ellington's creativity; new players stimulated his innovative urges.

Jimmie Blanton was only twenty years old when he came on the scene; yet he revolutionized string-bass jazz performance. Ellington put him out front and gave him honors as a soloist and joined him in recording some extraordinary piano-bass duets. Blanton's other great contribution was his approach to "walking bass," with strong accents on beats two and four. This emphasis "for the first time syncopated the foundation of the groove, creating great tension and driving forward motion."[1]

Tenor saxophonist Ben Webster was another addition. The mark of these two new members on the orchestra was so strong that the years 1939–1941 have become known as "the Blanton-Webster years." Memorable recordings from that period include "Jack the Bear," "Cotton Tail," "Ko-Ko," "Conga Brava," "What Am I Here For?" and "Concerto for Cootie," which became the popular 1943 vocal "Do Nothin' Till You Hear From Me." Webster stayed with the band until August of 1943, then returned in 1948. Blanton's star was bright but flickering; he contracted tuberculosis and had to leave the band, then died less than a year later, at the age of twenty-four. Ellington kept Blanton on the payroll during his illness, and later he took care of some expenses for Jimmie's mother and railroad transport of his casket.[2]

There were other losses, too. Growl trumpet player Cootie Williams left to play with Benny Goodman. (He returned some years later.) Barney Bigard, who played New Orleans-style clarinet, decided that he had been on the road long enough. Ivie Anderson and Herb Jeffries, two of Ellington's best vocalists, stayed on the West Coast after the 1941 production of *Jump for Joy*. Valve trombonist and copyist Juan Tizol, who wrote "Caravan" and "Perdido," also settled in California. Such turnovers were to be expected, but in Ellington's band players were not interchangeable. He wrote for the individual—not for the instrument. Ellington knew each player's strengths and he was able to bring those strengths out. He could even see weaknesses as beloved idiosyncrasies and as challenges that helped him create. He listened to the distinctive tone, range, or style of each of his sidemen and used those characteristics imaginatively in the music. Joining the Ellington band was like enlisting for an extended tour of duty; people stayed for years, for decades.

When anyone left the band there was a big void to fill, and often pieces were dropped from the repertoire because the man for whom they were written was no longer playing them. Personnel changes, then, required a new creative spurt and special attentiveness from the Maestro. Often he hired someone completely unlike the person who had left. Ray Nance, for example, joined the trumpet section after Cootie Williams. But Nance wasn't asked to attempt the growl trumpet sounds—instead, Ellington used Nance's other talents and his skill as a jazz violinist. Nance was such a natural entertainer that his nickname was "Floorshow." Harold "Shorty" Baker and Mercer Ellington also came into the trumpet section, but neither of them was a substitute for Cootie. On alto saxophone, Johnny Hodges' role became more and more prominent. He was a great blues player, but his sustained, satiny tone and lyrical embellishments on ballads were unmatched.

Just as Ellington could use his players' limitations as a goad to his creativity, he also had a way of turning obstacles into steppingstones. Two disputes became major problems for composers and for big bands in the early 1940s. The American Society of Composers, Authors, and Publishers (ASCAP) became embroiled in a dispute with radio stations, which in January 1941 resulted in a ban on playing the music of ASCAP members. Ellington's music couldn't be played—with resultant loss of income. But Mercer and Billy were not members. Strayhorn wrote "Day Dream," "Passion Flower," "Chelsea Bridge," and "After All"; and Mercer contributed "Moon Mist," "Blue Serge," and "Things Ain't What They Used to Be." The latter briefly served as the band's new theme song when "East St. Louis Toodle-O" had to be retired because of the ban. Later Strayhorn's "Take the 'A' Train" became the signature of the band, and remained so from then on. To further complicate business, in 1942 the American Federation of Musicians imposed a ban on recording—a decision that precipitated another major change in the popular music scene, as star vocalists came into ascendancy. During these years Ellington spent time on the West Coast making "soundies," short features, and the full-length MGM movie *Cabin in the Sky*. A short-lived collaboration with Orson Wells was profitable, though it ultimately was scrapped.

Duke's appearances in these films, especially the ones during the 1930s and early 1940s, endeared him to black moviegoers. He stood above the crowd in being able to present himself relatively free of demeaning stereotype, and his music often created an oppositional subtext in Hollywood productions that traded on distorted and shallow depictions of African-American life. While he was on the West Coast, Ellington brought to light another dream from his full basket. For years he had wanted to do a musical with an all-black cast. At a rollicking pre-dawn party at the Hollywood Hills home of screenwriter Sid Kuller, *Jump for Joy* was conceived and substantially funded by the gathering of celebrities, writers, and musicians there. Ellington had been playing the piano, and it was his comment on the celebration that provided the title for an all-black musical revue.

With stars such as Dorothy Dandridge, Herb Jeffries, Ivie Anderson, and Joe Turner, the musical comedy upended every demeaning Hollywood stereotype of African Americans and lampooned Jim Crow and other relics of white racism. The song "I've Got a Passport from Georgia" (and "I'm sailing for the U.S.A.") prompted death threats and was removed from the score. Ellington wrote all the music. The main lyricist was Paul Francis Webster, but the production involved numerous collaborators. The show was popular and played for twelve weeks in Los Angeles. The cast of sixty was exuberant over this unprecedented, heady freedom to be themselves and hoped it would go from there to Broadway or at least on the road, as did the producers and writers. But for a combination of reasons, the show

Duke Goes to the Movies

Black and Tan featured Ellington virtually playing himself as a composer whose livelihood is earned leading a band in a place much like the Cotton Club. All the music in this RKO 1929 movie short was his work, and the cast was all black. In *Check and Double Check* (1930) Ellington and the orchestra played his original compositions such as "Ring Dem Bells," and "Old Man Blues," a wry comment on Kern and Hammerstein's "Ol' Man River" from the 1927 stage musical *Showboat*. Film work in the early 1930s included *Bundle of Blues* with Ellington vocalist Ivie Anderson and two female dancers. In the full-length film *Murder at the Vanities* (1934) the Ellington orchestra is machine-gunned by a classical conductor outraged at their "jazzing up" the Second Hungarian Rhapsody by Franz Listz. (Ellington didn't write the music for this piece, although he and Strayhorn later did reinterpretations of suites by Tchaikovsky and Grieg.)

Ellington's most remarkable film in the early years was *Symphony in Black* (1935). Conceptually the film is shaped by Ellington's musical ideas and dominated by Duke's self-concept as a composer. (The young Billie Holiday, singing a blues number, was introduced to movie audiences.) As a suite of nine minutes, the music was Ellington's longest composition to that date.

The Hit Parade (1937) also featured performances by the Ellington Orchestra during a time when Hollywood studios were scrambling to sign up highly popular big bands. That same year Ellington appeared in a Paramount movie newsreel that presented him with great respect as the Maestro conducting "Daybreak Express." This is a sophisticated, harmonically complex piece inspired by the various sounds of a fast-moving train. Ivie Anderson joined the band for "Oh Babe! Maybe Some Day" in this behind-the-scenes look at record manufacturing technology.

Cabin in the Sky, released in 1943, was a major MGM film aimed at presenting a modern morality play with black characters. The story of "Little Joe" and his slouching progress toward heaven is presented through the technique of a long dream sequence framed by "real" events. Ellington and his band play at Jim Henry's Paradise Café, the site of the near-fatal shooting of the central character, played by Eddie "Rochester" Anderson. In a dream "Little Joe" sees his soul claimed by both God and the Devil, who agree that if the wounded hero can stick to the straight and narrow path for six months, he will find himself upward bound when his time comes. In *Jammin' at the Margins* Krin Gabbard argues that Ellington intentionally uses his music to subvert the film's ostensible premise, particularly with his choices of a "preaching" trombone soloist (the straight-laced Lawrence Brown), a musical convention associated with the church (call-and-response), and the title for the piece "Goin' Up." According to this analysis, the movie was already marked by self-contradiction in director Vincente Minnelli's mixing of opposed "urban" and "folkloric" views of Negro life. In the tradition of *Green Pastures*, the story line of *Cabin in the Sky* appears to advocate the virtues of faith and adherence to religious preachments while warning against a dissipated life of drinking, gambling, fighting, and carousing in clubs like Jim Henry's. But the film doesn't present its case convincingly, especially since the music-makers and joyful dancers at the Paradise Café seem to possess a more heavenly grace.[3]

Ellington also appeared in several "soundies," short-lived precursors of MTV that enabled juke-box customers to see as well as hear a popular tune. The Ellington soundies featured singers such as Herb Jeffries performing "Flamingo," Ivie Anderson in "I Got It Bad and That Ain't Good," and tenor saxophonist Ben Webster on "Hot Chocolate" (also titled "Cotton Tail"). There were several other orchestra appearances on film in the late 1940s and early 1950s, but none approached the significance of earlier work.

Anatomy of a Murder, a 1959 Otto Preminger film starring Jimmy Stewart, Lee Remick, and Ben Gazzara, was Ellington's first opportunity to write a full-length film score. He also made a brief on-camera appearance as "Pie Eye," playing piano at the hotel in the film's setting of the upper Michigan peninsula. His keyboard skills were employed for the dubs of Jimmy Stewart's playing as well. The film score, written collaboratively by Ellington and Strayhorn, won three Grammy awards that year.

Ellington and Strayhorn had another opportunity to do a film score for the 1961 film *Paris Blues*, starring Paul Newman, Sidney Poitier, Joanne Woodward, and Diahann Carroll. Louis Armstrong appears as a trumpet player named "Wild Man" Moore. Ellington also wrote a score for *Assault on a Queen*, a 1966 romp for Frank Sinatra. A film called *Change of Mind* (1968), about the transplant of a white man's brain into a black man's skull, also featured an Ellington score.

Ellington's popular songs, of course, are heard in other movies. But his presence on film comes full circle when he is depicted in Francis Ford Coppola's 1984 drama *The Cotton Club*. The romantic story line is predictably dark, complicated by the heroine's association with the underworld and by the psychologically tortured, dangerous lives of mobsters who controlled the Prohibition-era clubs. But Duke remains handsome, young, and commanding in a key venue of his early career, and the flashy floorshows seem like technicolor parallels of the monochrome dance sequences in the 1929 short *Black and Tan*.

was never repeated. This was a great disappointment to Ellington, who recorded some of the music, including the enduring hit "I Got It Bad and That Ain't Good," and "Rocks in My Bed."

With the entry of the United States into World War II, big bands faced some particular challenges. Ellington was too old to be in combat, but he was one of many who entertained the troops and promoted the sale of war bonds. Band ranks were thinned as players were drafted; gasoline was being rationed so that touring was drastically reduced; and some materials needed to make records were also required for purposes related to defense. Yet the music produced and played during the Swing Era helped keep Americans loving, dancing, and hoping through their own losses. The songs that came out of the Ellington orchestra shine in that constellation of American standards. There was "Sophisticated Lady," "In a Sentimental Mood," "It Don't Mean a Thing," "Solitude," "In a Mellotone," "Caravan," "I Let a Song Go Out of My Heart," "Jeep Is Jumpin'," "I Got It Bad," "Prelude to a Kiss," "C-Jam Blues." Ellington came home one day and announced to his sister Ruth, "We're going into the music publishing business, and you are the president." Tempo Music was founded in 1941, and the first songs published were Juan Tizol's "Perdido," Strayhorn's "Take the 'A' Train," and "Flamingo," with lyrics by Edmund Anderson.

While writing such popular songs, managing his business affairs, and dealing with the challenges specific to his career as a bandleader, Ellington's aspirations to take on larger and more serious compositional work had not diminished. In 1943 he had the opportunity to see another dream realized. He had long wanted to present a portrait of his people that would evoke the majesty of their achievement from their capture in Africa to their achieving a place of dignity within the American continent. The grandeur of the American Negro—and he used the word Negro—was the taproot of Ellington's artistry. He never became enamored of the pan-Africanism of the Harlem Renaissance nor of a similar trend in the 1960s; he admired the polyrhythmic elements of African music, but he distinguished between them and the rhythmic conventions of black Americans. While he was sympathetic to African independence from European colonialism, and celebrated this in works such as *The Liberian Suite*, his own identity was thoroughly and proudly American. This in no way meant he was insensitive to how long and how thoroughly citizens of color had been denied the freedoms associated with democracy in the United States. Despite that denial, he understood the triumph of a people who, under these constraints, retained the freedom to work, love, and pray; who bore arms and died for ideals that were denied them; and who danced out the meaning of life and sang away their sorrow. In *Black, Brown and Beige*, these were the themes he wanted to evoke.

This dream may have had its genesis in his schoolboy days in Washington. Tucker has identified two presentations as possible sources of inspiration for Ellington's concept. One was the pageant *The Star of Ethiopia*; the other a musical production called *The Evolution of the Negro in Picture, Song, and Story*, whose structure has much in common with *Black, Brown and Beige*. Certainly the idea was in his mind at least a decade earlier, when he was making the 1935 movie *Symphony in Black*, subtitled "A Rhapsody of Negro Life." The four vignettes of the film are tied together with scenes of Ellington composing the music at his piano, then appearing in an impressive concert hall and conducting the music for an elegantly dressed white audience. The opening scene that sets up the rationale for the movie is simply a letter which reads: "Just a reminder that the world premiere of your new symphony of Negro Moods takes place two weeks from today. . . ."[4]

Ellington was talking about such a work in the summer of 1938. At that time Ruth, accompanied by a chaperone, had gone abroad to supplement her graduate education at Columbia Teachers College. And Duke had gone into the hospital for a minor operation at the recommendation of his new physician, Dr. Arthur Logan. While he was convalescing Duke told interviewers about his "African suite," to be written in five parts. It was, he said, "just short of completion."[5] The occasion and impetus to write this envisioned suite came when Ellington made his Carnegie Hall debut in January 1943. The "African suite" idea took shape as a three movement work—almost an hour long—that he called *Black, Brown and Beige*. The concert included other well-known Ellington works, with *Black, Brown and Beige* presented at the end.

Ellington called this composition a "tone parallel to the history of the Negro race." In each of the three major movements were segments, such as "Work Song," "spiritual theme," "Light," "West Indian Dance," "Emancipation Celebration," and "The Blues." Ellington completed the work in about six weeks. A preview performance was given at a high school in Rye, New York. The extended work mystified audience and critics. Representatives of high culture thought it fell far short in an effort to mimic forms from the Western symphonic tradition. Those who included jazz within the realm of art, however, thought Ellington was mistakenly abandoning the things he did best. Within the reactions ranging from sad bewilderment to scathing criticism of his "pretensions," only a few voices offered favorable response. *Black, Brown and Beige* was performed in Boston Symphony Hall shortly thereafter, but Ellington relinquished his hopes that the composition would be a masterwork in his repertoire.

Rather than subject himself to further embarrassment, Ellington simply took parts of the work and used them in others ways.

The "spiritual theme" from the first movement had been inter-preted by Johnny Hodges with support from Ray Nance on pizzi-cato violin playing over a chorale-like orchestral foundation. The supreme alto saxophonist's sinuous yet lyrical tone reached from earth to heaven and back again in long, sustained phrases full of reverent aspiration. This thirty-two-bar ballad in AABA form sur-vived intact and eventually was titled "Come Sunday."

Black, Brown and Beige demonstrates that frequently Elling-ton had a visual image or a remembered experience in mind when he was composing. And if he didn't, he would sometimes create one after the fact, especially when he was presenting a retitled piece. Some of his most powerful writing came from attempts to recast a visual or aural impression in the idiom of music, a practice he and Bubber Miley had experimented with. "Eerie Moan," Ellington said, attempted to capture the sounds of human cries in the city at night, and "Warm Valley" came from the sight of voluptuous hills that reminded Ellington of the reclining female form. "Little African Flower" came from his imaginary vision of a beautiful flower blooming "only for God" in the heart of an impenetrable jungle.

Ellington had a picture in mind for "Come Sunday" as well, as his papers at the Smithsonian suggest. He was thinking of an African man named Boola, who is brought to the American con-tinent as a slave. He painstakingly teaches himself to read from a Bible. And there he finds "something to live for," even in his state of captivity; for he learns of a God of compassion and justice who knows his pain and will bring comfort and vindication. The pic-ture that Ellington imagines is a secret outdoor gathering of slaves on Sunday morning, while their white masters are in church. Together they share the word of God "in whispers" and long for the freedom openly to express their profound love and joy.[6] "Come Sunday" captures this feeling of poignant hope rising out of sorrow—not only the sorrow of slaves—but the tragic sense of life that all human beings face when they recognize their guilt and mortality. The song evokes a longing for some good beyond that end, and its simple beauty is like a slender thread of hope.

In *Black, Brown and Beige* Ellington created a tone parallel not just to the history of his race, but of the human race. The raw elements of life are all there: work, worship, sorrow, love, and play. Unfortunately, Ellington's complex compositional style was not as appreciated then as it was to become through study and performance after his death. Although there are still some who say that Ellington overreached his abilities with this effort, others defend the work as a daring attempt to incorporate jazz forms as well as harmonies, rhythms, and melodic themes to create an extended work. This was a significant departure from the more common practice of infusing classical forms with elements of jazz, as did European composers who were Ellington's contemporaries.

But if *Black, Brown and Beige* is the closest Ellington came to writing a symphony, then "New World A-Comin'" could be called his piano concerto, and it sometimes is. The piece was premiered at Carnegie Hall in December of that same year. The title "New World A-Comin'" was taken from a popular book by Roi Otley, a Harlem newspaperman who wrote optimistically about the future for black Americans. After each war in the nation's history, African Americans who fought and died for their country had hopes that afterwards they would be granted the full privileges of citizenship. Hopes were high in the 1940s that the freedoms and rights being defended in World War II would at last be extended to black Americans. In his spoken remarks when performing "New World A-Comin'," Ellington echoed Otley's optimism, but Duke's vision is all-encompassing: " 'New World A-Comin' " is a place in the distant future . . . where there will be no war, no greed, no categorization, no nonbelievers, where love is unconditional, and there is no pronoun good enough for God."[7]

Annual Carnegie Hall appearances in the 1940s and 1950s were spurs to more writing across categorical boundaries. Composing was only one of Duke's careers, however. Leading and managing a band was the other. In a three-part *New Yorker* profile, "The Hot Bach," Boyer captured many previously unknown elements of such a life and provided an extraordinary view of Ellington's personal schedule and habits, his collaboration with Strayhorn, the offstage amusements of the band members. There is also a retrospective angle, as Ellington reflected on his life up to that point. He is frank about the role of faith during the grief after his parents' death and the subsequent adverse affects on his work. He also talked about the rejuvenation of trips to Europe. It was like waking up in a new world, he said, where his freedom to come and go was unhindered, like eating caviar after a lifelong diet of hot dogs.

Ellington continued to stand against many challenges, but he and his players began to show signs of fatigue and even boredom with their work. Bebop musicians such as Dizzy Gillespie and Charlie Parker were heading a new creative thrust in jazz, and big bands never regained their pre-war level of popularity. Singers had captured the public's favor: stars such as Frank Sinatra, Ella Fitzgerald, Jo Stafford, Peggy Lee. Ellington liked to employ a retinue of singers and use them individually like another instrument. Al Hibbler, Herb Jeffries, Joya Sherrill, Marie Ellington (no relation), Kay Davis, Betty Roché, Ivie Anderson, and many others who stayed with the band for shorter periods, were fine performers with distinctive talents. But none of them acquired the status of a major star. Moreover, some of Ellington's best songs were difficult to sing, and the quality of added lyrics, with few exceptions, infrequently matched the musical artistry. A notable exception was the hit "I'm

Beginning to See the Light," with clever lyrics by Don George and a great interpretation by the teen-aged Joya Sherrill. (Harry James was listed as a co-composer, and he also recorded the song.) The title became a shorthand message of hope about victory in the war being fought on European and Asian fronts.

There was a futile attempt to revive *Jump for Joy* for a Miami performance, and Ellington also wrote the music for *Beggar's Holiday*, which recast a 1728 *Beggar's Opera* by John Gay into the tale of a modern gangster. The cast was racially integrated and the depictions free of stereotype; though it received some praise from critics, the show closed after fourteen weeks. There were other projects that might have become the Broadway musical Ellington dreamed of—a musical score for Shakespeare's *Timon of Athens*, one for *Murder in the Cathedral* by T.S. Eliot, and a comic opera called *Queenie Pie*. In 1965 Ellington completed a score for a show based on the Marlene Dietrich feature, *The Blue Angel*. Originally called *Sugar City*, later it was titled *The Pousse Café*. The songs have been performed, but Ellington never saw his dream of a Broadway musical realized.

Later in the decade of the 1940s, the band began receiving criticism from former admirers, and Ellington was advised to pack it in when the band gave a lackluster performance in an early television show. Duke didn't set foot in a recording studio for almost two years; there was another musicians' union ban and Columbia was not showing any interest. A European tour was limited to a small ensemble, when restrictions on foreign bands prevented the whole orchestra from performing.

Alexandre Rado first saw Duke in 1948, when Ellington toured with Ray Nance and Kay Davis, but he had heard the early Ellington band when he was about twelve or thirteen, listening to his brother's jazz records. "The Ellington things I heard were completely different . . . I found the music marvelous," he said. They became the first records Rado ever bought. Later, while managing his career in maritime trade, he produced many records with Ellingtonians. When the whole orchestra returned to Europe in 1950, Rado's early impressions were confirmed. "The musicians adopted me, became almost my second family," he said. He lived with the orchestra and produced its records, but he found Ellington to be unpredictable: "Nobody knew exactly what Ellington was." There was the man on stage, "putting in his pocket the public," and the man in rehearsal, "wearing an old hat and an old pullover with a hole in it."

Rado had a role in later productions of the sacred music in Europe; but even two decades earlier, he had seen evidence of Ellington's faith. "I know he was quite religious," Rado said. He was aware that Duke spent time alone in his room, thinking. "I know he was reading the Bible from the influence of his mother. He was keeping his mother's faith." It was through his music, Rado said, that Ellington showed his religious feeling, which he probably had all his life. "He could hardly understand that someone could not believe." He had a deep and strong belief—according to Rado—yet remained very open-minded in his religious thinking. "I liked his freedom of thinking in this respect, his idea that 'every man prays in his own language.'"[8]

The return to the Continent gave Duke new inspiration. He became more outspoken about his convictions on race relations and the need to end segregation, and he received an audience with President Harry Truman, who had dismantled the racial division of the country's armed forces. Ellington expected more in the way of an active civil rights agenda on the President's part, but Southern Democrats were in revolt in 1948, creating significant pressures against such a move. The composition that Ellington presented President Truman, "Harlem," a tone poem, was commissioned by Arturo Toscanini for the NBC Symphony Orchestra. The Ellington band's premiere performance of the piece was at a benefit concert for the NAACP in early 1951.

For the next several years Ellington kept going by sheer will and the income from royalties on his compositions and recordings. Then Johnny Hodges, along with Sonny Greer and Lawrence Brown, left the orchestra in early 1951. Hodges' solo work was a hallmark of the band; Greer had been by his side from the beginning. Brown provided that sweet trombone sound whose elegance and class contrasted so effectively with the plunger-mute strokes of Quentin Jackson.

Ellington responded with the "great James robbery." Drummer Louie Bellson, alto saxophonist Willie Smith, along with returning Juan Tizol, were lured away from the Harry James Orchestra. Duke retired some of the pieces that featured Hodges and added some of Bellson's compositions and spectacular solo drumming. There were other personnel changes, among them the addition of trumpeter Clark Terry—and the veteran reed players Harry Carney, Russell Procope, clarinetist Jimmy Hamilton were joined by tenor saxophonist Paul Gonsalves, with Smith in place of Hodges.

Ellington made some television appearances and began to explore the potential of long-playing records. He left Columbia and signed with Capitol; in his first Capitol recording session Duke made his 1953 hit "Satin Doll." Subsequently Capitol released an LP called *The Duke Plays Ellington*, a collection of piano solos with only bass and drums accompaniment. The collection, later retitled *Piano Reflections*, included "Reflections in D" and "Melancholia." The perseverance and the resilience demonstrated by Ellington came from his passionate artistic desire; he lived to write and to perform. The orchestra was essential to both: He needed what he called his "expensive gentlemen" not only to interpret his music, but to inspire him—and they needed him. For anyone who had played with Duke Ellington, there was no comparable musical experience; some of them left only to return to the setting where they could be themselves most fully. So it was with Johnny Hodges; by 1955 he was back in his old chair—and Duke Ellington was still dreaming.

Billy Strayhorn takes charge. (Courtesy Duke Ellington Collection, Archives Center, NMAH)

Lawrence Brown, trombone; Harry Carney, bass clarinet; Russell Procope, clarinet. (Courtesy of Dr. Theodore Shell)

Growl trumpet player Cootie Williams. (Courtesy of Dr. Theodore Shell)

Duke circa 1965. (Courtesy Dance Collection, Yale Music Library)

7

Rebirth, Rejection, and Sweet Revenge

The reward of a thing well done, is to have done it.

—*Ralph Waldo Emerson*

BY THE MID-1950S, rhythm and blues and rock and roll were replacing swing as popular music. The few surviving big bands scrambled harder to play what venues still existed. Bebop had given way to other modernist trends, bringing about a proliferation of styles and camps in jazz. Vocalists who kept elements of jazz styling occupied an island somewhere in the midst of a musical river that was diverging into distinct and separate streams.

The Duke Ellington Orchestra continued to travel the country, but many of the ballrooms and theaters they formerly played had closed. There were few long bookings, and they no longer traveled by train; a bus carried the players and other personnel. Harry Carney drove the car that carried Duke. Harry didn't do much talking, and this arrangement gave the Maestro some solitude. At times, when members of his family traveled with him, the long drives provided an opportunity to learn more about "Uncle Edward," as even his grandchildren called him.

Ellington continued to experiment with new forms and style, two notable examples were the piano solo called "The Clothed Woman" and an orchestral piece titled *Night Creature*. Critics continued to debate the relative merits of Ellington's early and later work. They tried to define, analyze, and assess the influence of his unique collaborative relationship with Billy Strayhorn. Ellington was still held in high esteem. He had become a virtual one-man institution in the jazz world and an international celebrity. In 1952 *Down Beat* magazine devoted an entire issue to Ellington in honor of the twenty-fifth anniversary of his career, dating from his 1927 opening at the Cotton Club. There were feature articles in other major publications as well. *Time* magazine was planning to do a cover story on Ellington, to be written by music editor Carter Harman. Peter Hurd was commissioned to paint Ellington's portrait.[1]

When Ellington had his portrait painted for the *Time* magazine cover story, the artist wrote Otto Fuerbringer, assistant managing editor, a handwritten letter describing the experience in detail.[2]

Dear Otto[:]

The Ellington episode was most interesting and the Duke, once he was badgered and harried enough by his agent posed patiently each afternoon for four days. I think he even enjoyed it for he stayed much longer the final day than was necessary for the completion of the portrait.

There was a more or less steady stream of phone calls and visitors to the hotel room where we worked and though I had known for years that California is over its quota in strange individuals I was amazed at the numbers and variety that turned up in my quarters to pay homage (of a sort) to the Duke. I was delighted for they served to entertain him and keep his expression animated during the sittings. . . .

I made friends with many of the musicians and with Al Celley the manager who was invaluable to me. On my last night in San Francisco I was invited by the Duke to a party he was giving after the concert at a place called Jimbo's Bop

City. This was great fun—a party I'll never forget: we sat eating roast turkey followed by watermelon until 6:30 a.m. while
a frenzied six-piece colored orchestra seemed to pound my
eardrums to ribbons—Say man, this cat really has had it! . . .

In spite of this attention, Ellington's characteristic resilience
and optimism were at a low ebb. The grind of his road appearances and the financial strain of those years were burdensome.
In 1955 Ellington was reduced to accepting a six-week engagement accompanying the Aquacades in Queens, New York, where
the management saw fit to add strings, harpists, and another
conductor for part of the show. But those years spawned the outdoor jazz festival as a new venue for many performers, both vet-
erans and newcomers. The granddaddy of them all was a series
George Wein produced at Newport, Rhode Island—a setting of
grand mansions and genteel New England manners not at all
like the urban scenes in which jazz began.

At the 1956 festival Duke Ellington appeared on July 7, the
last night of the event. After opening for some newer groups,
Duke and his men were to close out that night's show. He fumed
as the crowd of about seven thousand began thinning out, but
they finally took the stage at 11:45. His memory prodded by an
intermission conversation with George Avakian about some of
his early work, Duke decided to perform "Diminuendo and
Crescendo in Blue," written in 1938 but not performed in recent
years. The opening and closing sections are complex, but the
middle was simply a blues form, which any jazz musician can
improvise on. Tenor saxophonist Paul Gonsalves, who didn't
know the piece, was tapped to solo. Duke barked out the key and
promised to bring him in and take him out: "Just get out there
and blow your tail off. You've done it before."[3] That's exactly
what Gonsalves did, and the performance is remembered as one

of the most sensational events in jazz history. Avakian, who was recording the concert, tried to describe what happened, as did others; but no one can explain it.

The band began with a piece written especially for the occasion; then Duke opened "Diminuendo and Crescendo" with four rhythmic choruses. Duke was punctuating his piano playing with gutteral murmurs and shouted exclamations. Out of the crowd's sight, Count Basie's drummer Jo Jones egged on the rhythm section by slapping a rolled-up newspaper against the stage. The band answered, Duke came back for two more choruses to set up Gonsalves. Paul took over, always in sync with the driving rhythm behind him. At about the seventh chorus, the crowd began to catch fire, too. A platinum blonde in a black dress began dancing in one of the box seats, recalled one witness. Couples broke into jitterbug, and soon all seven thousand fans were on their feet, dancing, cheering, clapping—but still listening to the phenomenal performance. The band and the crowd were one now and Gonsalves kept going and did not stop until he had played twenty-seven choruses of "blazing hot jazz." The baton was passed onto the band, and by the time William "Cat" Anderson's trumpet was in the stratosphere, they had played an unprecedented fifty-nine choruses. The producer and the police were worried about a riot and tried to get Ellington to stop right there. Duke wagged his finger at them, then shook his head and proceeded to cool down the crowd the same way he heated it up—with more music.

What his first European tour had done for the young Duke, Newport did for the middle-aged, reigning monarch. And Duke had a new quip to deflect any references to his age: "I was born," he would declare, "in 1956 at the Newport Jazz Festival." He also was happy to let everyone assume that the feature story in *Time*, which came out shortly thereafter, was in response to this success. However, Ellington's portrait had already been painted, and the article just needed the right "news peg" for its publication. These were provided by photographs of the Festival appearance and a three-paragraph opening describing the sensation.[4] *Ellington at Newport*, became Ellington's best-selling record, and Columbia was again his recording company.

Black gospel music, with all the vitality of fire-baptized blues, was gaining interest in the 1950s outside the churches where it began. The music was the outgrowth of the influence of Thomas A. Dorsey, who brought it into the black churches in the 1930s. As a blues guitarist called Georgia Tom, Dorsey was associated with the low-down music church leaders considered inimical to the spiritual welfare of their flocks. After the death of his wife and baby at childbirth, Dorsey had gone through a spiritual and emotional crisis. He wrote hymns, such as "Precious Lord, Take My Hand," which had the same evocative quality as the blues, prompting an emotional and physical response in the hearers. He was convinced that God wanted this music in the church. But spontaneous emotional response was then not considered proper worshipful behavior in the old-line black churches. After his conversion Dorsey symbolically "reunited the bluesman and the traditional black preacher" and a new type of black church music was born.[5] But the heirs of Dorsey's musical tradition drew firm lines about where and how and with whom they would perform. When Mahalia Jackson was invited to sing at the Newport Jazz Festival, concessions about alcohol and the observance of Sunday had to be made to comply with the teachings of her church. Normally gospel singers didn't perform with Saturday night revelers such as jazz musicians. But when it came to Duke Ellington, Mahalia made an exception. She was quoted as saying that she considered the Ellington orchestra to be, not a jazz band, but a "sacred institution."[6]

A Columbia recording studio was the site of an extraordinary meeting between Duke and Mahalia in 1958. The session had been initiated as much as two years earlier, when Ellington sent her the music without lyrics. Mahalia's voice was a compelling natural instrument that seemed to resonate in every cell of her ample body. Unhindered by any conceits or vocal technique, her sound could be huge, yet still tender. She was the epitome of "soul," and her devotion imparted depths of meaning to the most simple lyric. In this case the lyric was "Come Sunday," the spiritual theme of *Black, Brown and Beige*. The album was given the title of Ellington's extended piece, although only portions of it are heard. As an attempt to revive the original work, the record was disappointing. The collaboration with Mahalia is the record's most appealing aspect. The lyrics used in this session are copyrighted to Ellington, although there may have been some collaboration. With echoes of scripture and old hymn texts coupled with references to human toil and weariness, these words are superior to later versions that Ellington copyrighted. Also, this text is the only version that contains the title phrase, which itself is an important metaphor symbolizing the resurrection or eighth day.

The recording session was conducted with as much care as the enactment of a liturgy. Duke liked to record a singer's first take, believing that the emotional involvement would be diminished in repeated tries. With Mahalia, he treated this moment like a "sort of divine revelation."[7] At the end of the song, she couldn't quite let the melody die and began humming spontaneously, an extemporaneous prayer captured on record. Duke wouldn't allow Mahalia to sing "Come Sunday" again until the next day, when he asked her to come back and sing it for him personally. This she did, in a completely darkened studio, with absolutely no accompaniment. However, Ellington did add another experiment, when he asked Mahalia to sing the words of the Twenty-third Psalm against a subtle orchestral background. At the 1958 Newport Jazz Festival, Ellington, the orchestra, and Jackson shared the stage on opening night. Mahalia sang "Come Sunday" in a free, rubato style and an upbeat "Keep Your Hand on the Plow."

For more than a decade Ellington had been making annual appearances at Carnegie Hall, occasions he used to present music of "social significance," including *The Liberian Suite* in 1947. Going back to works such as "Black Beauty" and "Black and Tan Fantasy," the case for racial equality being made in Duke's idiom preceded by thirty years the African-American demands for civil rights at midcentury. The southern states, with state and local laws that denied voting rights, education, and public access for black citizens, became the focus of attention, but the movement ushered in changes nationwide. Historic events, personal acts of courage, and eloquent new voices of leadership united African Americans. Responses from the white population ranged from support of the black cause, to mean obstructionist tactics and vicious, even deadly, retaliation.

In 1954 a unanimous Supreme Court in *Brown v. the Board of Education* declared racial segregation in schools to be unconstitutional, demolishing the "separate but equal" concept instituted by the 1896 *Plessy v. Ferguson* ruling. Then a Montgomery, Alabama, department store employee named Rosa Parks was arrested for refusing to move herself and her packages to the back of a city bus when white riders came on board. In 1957, Arkansas Governor Orval Faubus used the National Guard to block the admission of nine black students to Little Rock's Central High School. Subsequently, President Eisenhower nationalized the Guard and brought in federal troops to enforce the court order mandating integration. While the country wrestled with its conscience and the consequences of unredressed grievances, attention was also focused on the space race. The Soviet Union launched Sputnik, the first space satellite, in 1957. The United States responded as if challenged to a duel. The tensions of the Cold War found an outlet in this competitive effort, which represented superior achievement in education, science, and technology.

For Ellington, there was a relationship between these two national concerns, as a piece in *The Duke Ellington Reader* reveals. No source of publication is given for a typescript called "The Race for Space." Ellington made some of his strongest statements on equality and freedom, saying, in effect, that success in the space race could not be claimed until the country effectively addressed its wrong thinking and practices related to racial identity. He also revealed that one of the attractions of jazz for him was its provision of a sphere of freedom. Here was an arena in which human differences became inconsequential in the quest of a common experience, namely making music. Moreover, he included religion, which "should be a shining example," as an area of public life also marred by division: "Catholics against Protestants against Jews and all of them against the Negro."[8]

Ellington's words, as well as his music, and his numerous benefits for the cause of social justice demonstrated his courage and his efforts to speak against hate and prejudice. Yet he was criticized for not taking part in marches or mass protests. "He was revolutionary, but not militant, in race," Ruth Boatwright said. " 'Show enough love; people will let you in.' he would say." Ellington may have grown tired of waiting for that welcome to be extended to his brothers and sisters, but he continued to let his art speak for itself. At that time he identified social protest and pride in the history of the Negro as the most significant themes of his music.

When Ellington had an opportunity in 1963 to state his case musically, love and black pride were both at the center of his message. A group of Chicago citizens organized an exposition to celebrate the centennial of the Emancipation Proclamation. For this occasion Ellington created a musical revue called *My People*, which expressed many of the ideas in *Black, Brown and Beige*, but in a more popular idiom. "Come Sunday" and "The Blues" were included in a show that combined dance and music with a narrated history from slavery up to the present, with emphasis on the many contributions of African Americans to the national life. A personal portrait of Duke's family life was titled "Heritage," or "My Mother, My Father." His people's religious faith was celebrated in new songs such as "Will You Be There?," "Ninety-nine Percent," and "Ain't But the One." Ellington introduced "David Danced Before the Lord," an uptempo version of the "Come Sunday" tune with lyrics based on a passage from the biblical book of II Samuel. Tap dancer Bunny Briggs was featured on this piece.

Contemporary events were addressed with "King Fit the Battle of Alabam'." This spinoff of a traditional spiritual substitutes Martin Luther King, Jr., in place of the Hebrew military leader Joshua. The biblical battle site of Jericho becomes Birmingham, where Sheriff "Bull" Connor had turned firehoses and dogs on peaceful demonstrators. The musical tale is not as dark as the actual events themselves. In the song a baby stares down an attacking dog and humor defeats threats of violence. To sum up the basic message of the whole show, Ellington wrote "What Color Is Virtue?" It was during rehearsals for the production that Ellington and Dr. King met for the first time. The two embraced like old friends and listened together to the piece dedicated to King's witness. The show's run encompassed the August 28 date of the massive and pivotal March on Washington led by King.

Earlier that year, the Ellington band had made an extended tour of Europe, including performances in Milan, Hamburg, Stockholm, and Paris. There he had an opportunity to record his 1955 composition *Night Creature*, which required hiring more musicians. These were supplied by the symphony and opera orchestras of these four cities, and the album *The Symphonic Ellington* was the result. In the fall the orchestra toured overseas again, this time under the sponsorship of the U.S. State Department. Ellington absorbed new sights and sounds in the Middle and Far East and India. He also had to respond to questions about racial oppression back home. One night Ray Nance remained seated during the playing of the national anthem. Then news came of the November 22 assassination of President John F. Kennedy. The band came home after the State Department cancelled the remainder of the trip.

Western Europe was the destination of another tour in early 1964, when their performances were telecast. The exposure and serious treatment of their music on this trip starkly contrasted with the minimal exposure afforded by American networks. However, CBS-TV crews traveled with the orchestra later that year on a tour of Japan, where Ellington changed the schedule to give a performance to benefit relief efforts after a major earthquake there. The CBS footage was presented on the Walter Cronkite series *The Twentieth Century*.

Impressions of the Far East, a four-movement suite inspired by the 1963 tour, was premiered when the band played in Europe the following January. It was recorded that year more than twenty times, but not issued commercially. Three of the four segments were featured in a Canadian Broadcasting Company show called "The Duke," recorded in September of 1964.[9] (This work, a collaboration between Ellington and Strayhorn, was expanded later into *The Far East Suite* and recorded under that title in 1966.) The 1964 trip included Switzerland, Germany, Sweden, Denmark, and the familiar territory of France and England. For French and British jazz fans, it was another rendevouz in a thirty-year love affair that showed no signs of cooling down. The

British magazine *Melody Maker* gave Ellington its highest honors as Musician of the Year and winner of both critics and readers polls in the big band, arranger, and composer categories.

After his amazing career of almost forty years, Ellington was still far more honored by the musical establishment abroad than at home. A film account of American jazz musicians living abroad reinforced this dichotomy in an ironic way. Ellington and Strayhorn wrote a powerful film score for the 1961 movie *Paris Blues*, but it is unlikely Ellington was aware that the film script would veer in a direction that gave jazz the brushoff as a serious art form. The story line was drawn from a novel about a romance between a black jazz saxophonist living in Paris and a black schoolteacher visiting from the States. When Ellington agreed to do the film score, he understood that the movie script was going to depart from the novel by developing a romance pairing the characters played by Paul Newman and Diahann Carroll. However, that intention, if originally there, was never realized.

Rather, the saxophonist and the schoolteacher, played by Sidney Poitier and Carroll, overcome their differing views of how to deal with prejudice (foreign exile versus engagement on the home front). The Paul Newman character, a trombonist named Ram Bowen (loosely based on a character in the novel), is paired with Lillian (Joanne Woodward), in the movie version a younger and more central character who has an affair with Bowen. A secondary theme of the film, about the place of jazz in relation to European artistic conventions, arguably provoked another musical counter-message by Ellington in the last part of the score.[10] When Bowen seeks endorsement of his talent as a composer from a major classical impresario, his work is dismissed as nothing more than a smattering of interesting melodies. Bowen decides to pursue the prescribed path (out of jazz) that will legitimate his talents. The following year Ellington was denied recognition for his compositional work in a controversial Pulitzer Prize decision.

In 1965 three new music jurors had been named by the Pulitzer Prize board, charged through the Columbia University School of Journalism with awarding prizes established through a gift by Joseph Pulitzer. The Board had been dominated for many years by Nicholas Murray Butler, the Columbia University president who obtained the gift. According to long-time Board secretary and prize administrator John Hohenberg, that year the Board and the University president were hoping that these three music critics—Winthrop Sargeant of *The New Yorker*, Ronald Eyer of *Newsday*, and Thomas B. Sherman of the *St. Louis Post-Dispatch*—would be bold in their recommendations and come up with a "new and highly original choice," beyond an accepted coterie of American composers who worked in traditional forms such as symphonies, concerti, and opera.[11]

The terms governing the music prize in 1965 stipulated that it be given "For a distinguished musical composition in the larger forms of chamber, orchestral or choral music, or for an operatic work (including ballet), performed or published during the year by a composer of established residence in the United States."[12] No music prize had been awarded the previous year. The new jurors judged that no such work was deserving of the prize that year. Instead, they unanimously proposed that a special citation be given to Ellington, not for a single work, but for his artistry and influence as a whole. Even this recommendation, however, carried a somewhat apologetic, defensive tone, when it suggested that Ellington's work, though "couched mainly in the idiom of jazz," had high artistic quality with "roots in the musical tradition of his race."[13]

In a cursory response, the Board rejected the jurors' recommendation for an "appropriate citation" on the grounds that it fell outside the terms of the award. A motion to forego a music award that year was unanimously approved and without debate. No one even bothered to discuss the value and originality of Ellington's compositions over three decades, Hohenberg wrote some thirty years later. The Board did not take the jurors' recommendations seriously, he said, because they went outside the guidelines of the prize at that time. However, a review of the Board's decisions in other areas reveals that such a general or special citation was by no means unheard of. As far back as 1941 *The New York Times* had received a Special Citation in Journalism for the overall value of its foreign news reporting. A Special Citation in Letters was awarded in 1961 to *The American Heritage Picture History of the Civil War.* Walter Lippmann was given the 1962 Pulitzer for International Reporting for his interview of Soviet Premier Khrushchev, "as illustrative of Lippmann's long and distinguished contribution to American journalism," a wording that suggests it was his career, more than this piece, which was being recognized. In 1964 Gannett Newspapers was recognized for using its group resources to complement the work of member publications. The program cited was "The Road to Integration."

Pulitzer Prize winners in all categories of American journalism, arts, and letters in 1965 were announced May 3. Meantime, the inside story on the music decision had been leaked to the press, presumably by the music jurors. Within days, *The New York Times* reported that the Pulitzer board had denied Duke Ellington a prize for his distinguished contributions in music. The outraged response in the press was overwhelming. "He's deserved it for so long," lamented Aaron Copland, whose *Appalachian Spring* ballet won the music prize in 1945. The *San Francisco Chronicle* called the Pulitzer board's action "an appalling insult."[14] Music jurors Eyer and Sargeant had resigned their positions in protest of the Board's action, while Sherman simply acknowledged that he had not been reappointed.

Ellington, predictably, was on the road with his band. With his enormous capacity for patience and trenchant irony, the sixty-six-year-old composer came up with a response that has since been widely quoted and variously understood: "Fate is being kind to me. Fate doesn't want me to be too famous too young." This statement prompted Hohenberg, remembering the incident in 1997, to cite Duke's exemplary grace and remember him as the occasion's hero. Others have received the ambiguous statement as a disarmingly philosophical comment, but it contains a barb with potent poison on the tip. Nat Hentoff, a respected writer about jazz and its makers, interviewed Ellington and band members for a *New York Times Magazine* article titled "This Cat Needs No Pulitzer Prize." The article celebrated Duke's freedom to do what he liked best, and he was quoted disclaiming any concern for recognition or reward other than the music itself.

By that time Ellington had received New York City's Bronze Medal from acting mayor Paul Screvane, whose citation praised Duke for having "captured the spirit of a time and of a whole nation" and maintained a "standard of perfection."[15] According to an account in *The New Yorker,* the ceremony included popular Ellington tunes played by a Department of Sanitation band and Joe Williams's singing of "Come Sunday." Attending the ceremony with Ellington were "Mrs. Ellington" (Evie Ellis), Dr. Arthur Logan, and The Reverend John Gensel, who was referred to as a "Lutheran missionary to the New York jazz community." The article also mentioned Ellington's recent recordings of tunes from the *Mary Poppins* score, some by the Beatles, and *Recollections of the Big Band Era.* Ellington had just premiered a new suite, *The Golden Broom and the Green Apple*, with the New York Philharmonic. An additional appearance was scheduled at Philharmonic Hall in a Great Performers series, followed by a December recital at Lincoln Center.

Paul Gonsalves, Money Johnson, and Harold Ashby. (Courtesy of Dr. Theodore Shell)

Duke relaxes with a friend. (Courtesy Duke Ellington Collection, Archives Center, NMAH)

In his article for *The New York Times Magazine*, Hentoff clicked off these coups and portrayed Ellington as the calm center of the storm, even while keeping the grueling one-nighter pace of one of the few big bands to have survived beyond the 1950s. Sitting with the writer at two o'clock in the afternoon, in a Rockford, Illinois, hotel room, Ellington was drinking his morning coffee. He placed himself above the fuss and fray while matter-of-factly—and colorfully—putting his finger on the sore spot. Jazz is still seen by most Americans, he said, as being like the kind of man you wouldn't want your daughter to associate with. "I'm hardly surprised that my kind of music is still without, let us say, official honor at home," he said as he cited European music as the standard still accepted by many Americans.[16] Thus Ellington exposed two prejudices at once and unmasked the boogyman fears behind resistance to integration.

It remained for the brilliant black novelist and essayist Ralph Ellison to decipher the subtext of Ellington's original public response. Ellison later wrote a tribute to Ellington, prompted by the occasion of the composer's seventieth birthday. This event was to be celebrated at a state dinner hosted by President Richard M. Nixon in the White House, where Ellington's father had served as a caterer and butler contracted for special occasions. Ellison noted that what the country's artistic institutions had failed to do was left to Presidents to rectify—not only Nixon, but also Lyndon Johnson, who had earlier hosted Ellington at the White House. The essayist recalled the Pulitzer controversy and Ellington's by then legendary statement about Fate being kind to him. This response was, Ellison said, a quip that mocked double standards, hypocrisies, and pretensions. He compared it to the dancing of slaves who began burlesquing the grave steps of their masters and then forced those steps "into a choreography uniquely their own."[17]

8

Wider Horizons

A riot is at bottom the language of the unheard.
—*Martin Luther King, Jr.*

THE DECADE OF THE 1960s was a time of major change not only in social and political life, but also in religion. Under the leadership of Pope John Paul XXIII, the Roman Catholic Church began internal reforms that also influenced other major Christian bodies in their worship and in their relations with each other. Since the end of World War II, major Protestant denominations (predominantly white) had been exploring ecumenical cooperation through the National Council of Churches and the World Council of Churches.

New translations of the Bible into modern English were published by groups of Protestant and Roman Catholic scholars. The language of the Catholic mass was changed from Latin into the national language of the parishioners in a given congregation. Vernacular music was also introduced into Catholic worship. Jazz masses and Protestant jazz services gained a degree of popularity in urban areas, although the practice was still seen as a radical departure from traditional worship. Prominent rabbis and Catholic bishops hosted radio and television shows or wrote syndicated newspaper columns. Protestant seminary professors such

Columbia University honorary doctorate, 1973.
(Courtesy Duke Ellington Collection, Archives Center, NMAH)

as Reinhold Neibuhr and Paul Tillich were well known to the public. Tillich's "theology of culture" identified artistic activity as crucial to the "radical spiritual task of disclosing the authentic nature of God in creation."[1] His influence led to renewed support and study of the arts within churches and seminaries.

These trends were part of the cultural atmosphere in 1965 when the Duke Ellington Orchestra presented A Concert of Sacred Music at Grace Cathedral in San Francisco, the seat of the Episcopal Bishop of California. At the conclusion of the Grace Cathedral concert, Ellington expressed his gratitude for this opportunity, which allowed him to express his faith in words and music. "I'm sure," he said, "that this is the most important statement we've ever made."

The imposing Gothic structure, modeled on the great cathedrals of France, had a magnificent setting on Nob Hill. The ambitious construction task took years, but long before completion, plans were being made for a year-long celebration called Festivals of Grace. Presentations of *Billy Budd* and *Long Day's Journey into Night* were scheduled, along with many other events reflecting the concerns and tastes of that era. The Archbishop of Canterbury and Eugene Carson Blake, head of the World Council of Churches, were to be guests. Professor Paul Tillich of Union Theological Seminary, in New York City, preached at the main Sunday morning liturgy on January 31.

Dr. Martin Luther King, Jr., had the previous year received the Nobel Peace Prize for his civil rights leadership. His preaching from the Cathedral's lofty pulpit on a Sunday in March drew a crowd that has never been matched since then.[2] Police security was extremely tight for his entire San Francisco visit, and there was great concern over the mob of people who were left standing outside because there was no more space inside. When they heard on the loudspeakers that the offering was being taken, they began to shout, "Where are the offering takers for out here? Send us the offering takers." "It was a testimony to the spirit of the people," said Dean Bartlett later. "They just wanted to be a part."[3] Dates for the concert by the Ellington orchestra were penciled into the Cathedral schedule for six months later, but in no way was Ellington's participation an afterthought.

Yet the concert might never have taken place if an Episcopal clergyman serving on the Bishop's staff had not been an Ellington devotee. Bishop James A. Pike was a controversial, liberal churchman who had lectured and preached around the country. The Dean of the Cathedral, C. Julian Bartlett was a native of New Orleans and enamored of its jazz tradition. The Reverend John S. Yaryan broached the idea of an appearance by the Ellington orchestra, and all agreed that the invitation should be issued. Ellington first heard of it in October of 1962, according to a letter written the following December by Canon Yaryan. During an engagement Ellington was playing in the San Francisco area, Canon Yaryan went to his dressing room between sets. Duke was lounging on a bed, his legs propped up against the wall. They chatted for a while, then Canon Yaryan gathered up his nerve to say, "Dr. Ellington, I'd like to tell you I'm here to commission you to compose and play a concert of sacred music at the completion of Grace Cathedral. . . . which will be about four years from now."[4]

Duke seemed astonished by this proposal, the cleric told an international meeting of Ellington scholars and fans. "I understand that one other person had seen him nonplussed. But can you imagine, slow motion, this wonderful, handsome man— those legs came down just so very, very slowly, and he sat up and looked me in the face: 'What did you say?' I repeated myself, and he never said, 'I will'; but he *inferred* that this was very exciting." Duke was slow to say "I will." A series of enthusiastic and increasingly solicitous letters were sent to him over several months'

A Memorable Meeting

The Reverend C. Julian Barlett was interviewed for an oral history by Cathedral archivist Michael Lampen some twenty years after Ellington's First Sacred Concert. These comments were excerpted from a transcript provided by the Cathedral Archives.

The first of Duke Ellington's Sacred Concerts took place here in the Cathedral. The Reverend John Yaryan, known among us as Jack Yaryan, was one of the bishop's canons—a canon to the ordinary—and he approached [me] one time and said that he had been a fan of Duke Ellington's for many, many years; and did I know that Duke Ellington had written quite a little few pieces of music of a religious import. I said, 'No, I never heard of such a thing.' He said, 'Well, it's true.' He said, 'I have a hell of an idea. Why don't you ask Duke Ellington to give a religious concert in Grace Cathedral?'

"And lo and behold, he accepted with alacrity and said that by happy coincidence he was scheduled to have a week's run at a dancing restaurant down the Peninsula. He would be glad to talk to Canon Yaryan at that time. We took our wives down and spent an evening in the restaurant. During every intermission, the Duke would come and sit at our table, and we'd take up our conversation again. Well, by that time, he had the whole idea of his concert worked out in his own mind—pieces that he would have and people that he wanted to bring here especially, and he was just so eager to have this done. He had never done anything like this in his life. So far as I know, it had never been done anywhere. So time marched on, and the . . . date was set, and he worked out his program. I can only remember two of the pieces, but they all had input, religiously speaking. It was magnificent.

"Of course, we had press notices ahead of time. The press flocked in here. He was a perfectly wonderful man, and he said in my presence at that press conference that he regarded this coming event to be the most significant musical statement he will have made in his life. His gratitude to us knew no bounds, and he charged us only the going union rate for his musicians—all of that he picked up. It cost him, I'm sure, thousands of dollars. He never even mentioned it. I asked him, of course, what this was going to cost us at early stages. He said, 'Now, Dean, I don't want you to worry about that. This is a privilege for me.'

"Well, we made sound friendships. For years, that man would send my wife—no matter where he was, anywhere in the country—he would send my wife a large bouquet of beautiful roses on Mother's Day. [At] Christmas he would send us half a case of champagne, or something. We were good friends 'til the day he died. I can't say enough about him."

119

time. There were questions about dates, the nature of the program, costs, and other details, but apparently no response from Ellington until almost two years later. Then Duke made a phone call and arranged for the clergymen and their wives to join him for conversation over dinner at a Redwood City restaurant and dance club where he would be playing.

Once Ellington's acceptance became official and plans were made, the event became a news item of great interest. *Time* magazine ran a story with a picture of Ellington with Bishop Pike, giving their rationale for this barrier-breaking event. Mail began coming in to the office of the Cathedral, requests for ticket information along with critical response. Someone clipped a copy of the *Time* article and wrote across it "Everything about this concert is disgusting." In all press releases and news conferences, the word jazz was scrupulously avoided. Ellington called these compositions "contemporary sacred music."

For this concert Ellington used a combination of previously composed numbers, including portions of *Black, Brown and Beige*. The Herman McCoy Choir flew in from Southern California and sang a group of spirituals. From *My People* there came "Ain't But the One" and "David Danced Before the Lord," with tap dancer Bunny Briggs and jazz singer Jon Hendricks. Toney Watkins sang a calypso-style version of "The Lord's Prayer" a cappella, and Duke played his 1943 piano composition "New World A-Comin'." Two gospel-style pieces were introduced by Esther Marrow, who sang "Come Sunday" in the soulful style of Mahalia Jackson. The showpiece of the event was "In the Beginning God," a fifteen-minute long composition that featured Hendricks, Harry Carney, Paul Gonsalves, Cat Anderson, drummer Louie Bellson, supported by the choirs and the rest of the band.

Ellington presented Esther Marrow in her Sacred Concert numbers and Jon Hendricks and Bunny Briggs in "David Danced" in a Sunday program at the Monterey Jazz Festival that same month. A somewhat altered version of the concert was performed twice on December 26 at the Fifth Avenue Presbyterian Church in New York City. After A Concert of Sacred Music, Ellington continued to present these pieces in other houses of worship, including Coventry Cathedral in England. Duke began to think of himself as "God's messenger boy," he said. As surprising as this opportunity was when it came, nothing could have been more appropriate or natural to Ellington as an expression of his largely private religious convictions. Now he could express "loudly and openly" what he had been saying quietly on his knees.[5]

While preparing for the concert at Grace Cathedral, Ellington had asked for prayers on behalf of Billy Strayhorn, who was undergoing surgery for cancer of the esophagus about that time. Duke had consulted Billy when he was composing a new piece for this event. From the West Coast he called Billy back in New York and asked him to think of a six-note theme corresponding to the six syllables in the phrase "In the Beginning God," the opening words of the biblical book of Genesis, King James Version. Ellington wrote his theme; Strayhorn wrote his. Both their melodies started and ended on the same note. In their individual six-note melodies, only two notes were different. After the San Francisco event, Strayhorn continued to decline. His composing did not stop, however. Pieces chronicling the course of his illness carried titles like "Blood Count" and "U.M.M.G." (Upper Manhattan Medical Group). What biographer Hajdu called Strayhorn's "dying scream" was "Suite for the Duo," a twelve-minute piece written for piano and French horn. Strayhorn wrote it after hearing Dwike Mitchell, piano, and Willie Ruff, bass and French horn, perform at the Hickory House in New York. The Mitchell-Ruff Duo recorded it, along with other Strayhorn compositions, in 1969.

Edna Ellington also was in failing health. Although she and Duke were separated, they remained in touch and, by several accounts, had a friendly relationship. Ellington supported her until she died. "Whenever Edna became ill, of course, Duke and Mercer and all of them and Ruth were in New York. And so they would take her up there and hospitalize her there because there he could keep tabs on her," explained June Norton, who knew both Edna and Duke through the years. With his estranged wife and Billy Strayhorn both gravely ill, Duke still called June when her son lost his life after an accident at school that year. Edna died in New York within days, then was buried in Washington.[6]

As Strayhorn wasted away, Ellington had to face an immense loss, probably the most difficult since the death of his parents. He was in Reno when his sister Ruth called to tell him of Billy's death. With soul-mate Lena Horne at his bedside, Billy died May 31, 1967. Duke's reaction was, understandably, to cry and beat his head against the wall, and ask "Why?" Then he sat down and wrote a loving tribute to his "favorite person," William Thomas Strayhorn, little Swee'Pea, the "biggest human being that ever lived."[7] He called the clergy friends who had been praying for Billy, told them of his death, and asked them to continue their prayers. Ellington published this tribute in his memoirs. Tucked in his description of Strayhorn's great musical gifts is one self-revealing sentence. Duke credited Billy as the inspiration for his own courage from the time the two had joined forces in the late 1930s. A musical remembrance came several months later, when a small group of Ellingtonians recorded the album *And His Mother Called Him Bill*. In the recording studio that day Duke played out his emotions in two powerful inter-pretations of Stayhorn's "Lotus Blossom."

In 1967 Duke was also preparing to present his Second Sacred Concert, which was commissioned by the Cathedral

Church of Saint John the Divine and scheduled for January 16, 1968. A performance of this music was done the previous April at the Mother A.M.E. Zion Church in Harlem.[8] The Second Sacred Concert consisted of all new material, although it shared some themes with the first concert. "Supreme Being" opens with an orchestral depiction of the chaos that existed before creation. The choirs then chant Ellington's paraphrase of Genesis 1 and 2. This was the first concert for Alice Babs, and she had some of Ellington's best music to sing. Cootie Williams was outstanding on a blues dedicated to Pastor John Gensel, "The Shepherd Who Watches Over the Night Flock." The longest piece was "It's Freedom," with many segments tied together by chorale-like singing by the choir. In the official premiere performance of the Second Sacred Concert, Strayhorn's presence and influence were still evident. In the performance at St. John's, Duke was visibly moved when he began a Strayhorn-inspired soliloquy in the middle of "It's Freedom." Duke enumerated the "four moral freedoms" which he attributed to Billy.

The two men were opposites in size and temperament, complementary in their musical skills.[9] Moreover, the two were united in a kind of marriage of the minds, in which both were attracted to personal qualities in the other that were less prominent in themselves.

In Strayhorn Duke perceived an equanimity, patience, and humility of spirit. So as Duke enumerated the four freedoms that Billy lived by, he probably was not quoting Strayhorn. Rather he was articulating what he had seen in the younger man's character and behavior, virtues that he wished he possessed in greater strength. By the time Duke wrote "The Majesty of God" for the Third Sacred Concert, the quality of humility had become so crucial that it was lifted up in the final line of the piece "The Majesty of God." The original conclusion of the piece is missing from the recorded version of the concert, which was edited for musical reasons. However, these words were in the program of the last Sacred Concert that Ellington presented December 23, 1973, at St. Augustine's Presbyterian Church in the Bronx, in New York City.[10]

From 1968 until 1973, Ellington continued presenting the Second Sacred Concert, or portions of it. News of the assassination of Martin Luther King, Jr., interrupted an April 4, 1968, Carnegie Hall performance, which included Sacred Concert music with the Tougaloo College choir. That weekend riots broke out in major urban areas, including Washington, where the old U-Street entertainment venues were one casualty of an explosion of black outrage. The country was divided on two different domestic issues in the year 1968. Civil rights leaders were focusing on economic justice. (King was in Memphis to lend support to striking garbage collectors.) Political divisions over the war in Vietnam had come to the fore and were central in the 1968 political campaigns. President Lyndon Johnson decided not to run for re-election and initiated peace talks in Paris.

When Robert F. Kennedy was shot and killed while campaigning for the Democratic presidential nomination the following June, Ellington and his white bassist, Jeff Castleman, appeared on a memorial tribute to the late senator. Later that month Duke announced the opening of a series of fifty concerts from a touring "Jazzmobile." Ellington had visited the White House several times during the administration of Lyndon Johnson. After police violently reacted to anti-war protesters during the 1968 Democratic Convention in Chicago, the convention nominated Vice President Hubert Humphrey, who had to assume the political liabilities of the Vietnam war. With former Alabama governor George Wallace as a third-party candidate, the extreme divisions within the country were brought into painfully sharp focus. Republican Richard Nixon in November gained the presidential office he had sought and lost to John F. Kennedy in 1960. Whatever Duke's personal reaction was to the political tensions of those times, the musical message he carried with him remained that of freedom, forgiveness, love, and unity. On one day in September 1969, he played Bishop James A. Pike's favorite hymn at a Requiem Mass at St. Clement's Episcopal Church and also did a benefit banquet for Muhammad University of Islam. The next day he was honored by New York City Mayor John Lindsay, and four days later his tunes enlivened a charity ball sponsored by the Des Moines (Iowa) Junior League.[11]

Whether in the White House or on the streets of Harlem, in supper clubs or on college campuses, Duke Ellington's music—particularly the Sacred Concerts—had great potential for linking people of different backgrounds, ethnicities, ages, religious persuasions, and political views. This potential was realized in a wonderful way in New Orleans in April 1970. The Duke Ellington Orchestra was playing at Al Hirt's Club for five nights before presenting the Second Sacred Concert as the last formal event of the Festival. The site was the Municipal Auditorium, where a similar program had been given two years earlier.

Kelly-Marie Berry, a young black woman teaching movement and dance at Tulane University, had the opportunity to choose dancers and to choreograph their performance for "Praise God and Dance." At the time she had white students in one class, and black students in another, which she offered unofficially. The latter had drawn black students from other colleges in the area. Out of those classes and the Sacred Concert project came the city's first interracial and intercollegiate dance group.

For the blockbuster "Praise God and Dance," Berry asked the students to ritualize a celebration of spring infused with the mystique of "voudon" culture associated with New Orleans history. The choreography, as it developed, was "spirit and flesh

Happy Birthday, Duke

After Richard M. Nixon became president in 1969, plans were made for a special celebration of Ellington's seventieth birthday. The banquet and bash were organized by Nixon aide Attorney Leonard Garment, who had played clarinet for Woody Herman, and Willis Conover of the Voice of America. Ellington's family and about fifty other guests joined White House invitees and their hosts, the President and Mrs. Nixon. Into the rooms where Ellington's father had once worked on special occasions as a butler or caterer, came guests such as Cab Calloway, Benny Goodman, Billy Eckstine, Dr. Arthur Logan, Ebony magazine publisher John Johnson, Labor Secretary George Schultz, accompanied by their wives. Some of the country's greatest jazz musicians were both guests and entertainers, among them Dave Brubeck, Dizzy Gillespie, Billy Taylor, Earl Hines, Milt Hinton, Clark Terry, Bill Berry, Paul Desmond, and Gerry Mulligan. Joe Williams did "Jump for Joy" from Duke's 1941 musical. Duke and Willie "the Lion" Smith sat in at the piano when Williams sang "Stormy Monday." The chandeliers were swinging and everyone was dancing, including Duke. The music went on until 2 a.m.

That evening President Nixon bestowed on Edward Kennedy Ellington the country's highest civilian award, the Presidential Medal of Freedom. The presentation included these words of tribute: "Duke is one who has carried the message of freedom to all the nations of the world through his music, through understanding, through understanding that reaches over all national boundaries and over all boundaries of prejudice and over all boundaries of language. Because he has that unusual gift, a gift that he has shared with us, his own fellow citizens, and with the citizens of the world, we believe that this citation fits him particularly well."

After thanking the president and the applauding guests, Duke responded.

"The word 'freedom' is one, coincidentally, that we are using at the moment in our Sacred Concert, and, of course, we speak of freedom generally . . . but at the end, when we get down to the payoff, what we actually say is that we would like very much to mention the four major freedoms that my friend and writing and arranging companion Billy Strayhorn lived by and enjoyed."

Then he gave President Nixon the Ellington four kisses, "one for each cheek," and the President, joking and laughing, sat down at the piano to accompany everyone's singing "Happy Birthday" to Duke "in the key of G, please."[12]

uniting," she explained many years later. The dancers embodied wood sprites, flowers, forest creatures with painted faces and voudon names, all joined to welcome spring and to praise God. She was concerned that this concept might not be in keeping with earlier performances or with Duke's ideas. Berry and the student dancers were invited by one of the Festival sponsors to meet and hear Ellington at the band's Club appearance. But when thirty people showed up, the invitation was rudely withdrawn. "How could you be so stupid to act upon a verbal invitation? The company is not going to pick up the admission tab for all these kids," said the enraged man.

Berry, at first at a loss, asked to see Ellington's manager. She and one of the dancers were enthusiastically welcomed by members of the Ellington staff and escorted backstage. His manager assured her that Ellington was aware that the dancers were at the club. He regarded the students as his personal guests. Ellington would pick up the admission tab and simply wanted the group to have a nice time. Between sets Berry was able to meet with Duke and discuss her ideas. He told her not to be anxious about how it had been presented by others in such places as San Francisco, New York, and Stockholm. "He quietly said, 'Just do it as you see it and believe in what you see,'" recalled Berry.[13]

New honors for the Duke seemed to be coming from every quarter. President Lyndon Johnson invited him to the White House on seven different occasions. Ellington performed at the White House Festival of the Arts in 1965, received the President's Gold Medal in 1966, and was appointed to the National Council on the Arts in 1968.

The Soviet Union was one destination of a tour in 1971, the same year that the Royal Swedish Academy of Music admitted Ellington to membership. He was the first nonclassical composer to be so recognized in the Academy's long history. Duke went to Boston to receive an honorary doctorate from the Berklee College of Music, where he had often been involved in its jazz education program. Columbia University, the institutional base of the Pulitzer Prizes, granted him an honorary doctorate. He received honorary degrees from Armstrong, the Washington high school he never graduated from, and major universities such as Yale, Brown, Howard, and St. Louis, which was one of the sites of a Sacred Concert. Christian Theological Seminary granted Ellington an honorary doctorate in humane letters. The University of Wisconsin invited him to visit in July 1972. He spent five days in residence there, holding master classes and giving concerts, including one with University choirs joining the orchestra to present the sacred music. Ellington had an ability to communicate with people of all ages and from all walks of life. For this Midwestern appearance he even wrote a polka titled "Klop," which became part of his *UWIS Suite*.

Ellington seemed to enjoy these exchanges with students and young musicians. In 1969 he took a short leave from his engagement at the Las Vegas Sahara Hotel to travel to the San Francisco Bay Area and play with the California Youth Symphony in a benefit at the Foothill College gymnasium. In his autobiography he paid tribute to a long list of jazz educators and the colleges where they were teaching. At the same time he was reaching back into his past, and the history of jazz. The legacy of various jazz influences was commemorated in *The New Orleans Suite*, which included portraits of Sidney Bechet, Wellman Braud, Louis Armstrong, and Mahalia Jackson, and a tribute to the "second line" of New Orleans funeral tradition. In sacred spaces Ellington played music originally written for performances in clubs or concerts, sometimes retitling them. In club engagements he was playing the music written for his worshipful Sacred Concerts.

Duke Ellington rarely performed solo piano concerts, although as a pianist he had exceptional skills and a distinctive style. One such unusual occasion took place as part of the Composers Showcase series at the Whitney Museum in New York City on April 10, 1972. Ellington brought along bassist Joe Benjamin and drummer Rufus Jones for good company, suggesting his preference for collaboration. The selections that night covered the full sixty-year span of Ellington's career, from "Soda Fountain Rag" of Washington adolescent days to "Black and Tan Fantasy" from the Cotton Club to the last popular hit born of the Strayhorn collaboration, "Satin Doll."

The special place he accorded his sacred music is reflected in his choosing at least five pieces from the Sacred Concerts for the evening's program. The recording lists these as "Meditation," "New World A-Comin'," "The Night Shepherd," and "Kixx," which featured Jones on a shortened version of "The Biggest and Busiest Intersection" from the Second Sacred Concert. Dan Morgenstern, jazz historian and director of the Institute of Jazz Studies at Rutgers University, described the evening in liner notes for a 1995 release of the recorded performance.

If I remember correctly, the large and enthusiastic audience was seated on risers—the Whitney not then having an auditorium sufficiently capacious for such an occasion. It included "Flamingo" lyricist and old friend and confidant Edmund Anderson, young Ellington amanuensis Brooks Kerr, right-hand man and noted critic Stanley Dance, and other notable Ellington friends, associates and admirers. The night before, many of us had been on hand not far from the Whitney, at St. Peter's Lutheran Church, to witness a performance of Ellington's most recent version of his "Sacred Concert." This had taken place the day after the band's return to New

York from a seven-week tour of the U.S., which had begun immediately upon their completion of a thirty-six-day odyssey that took them from Japan to Taiwan to the Philippines to Hong Kong to Thailand to Burma to India to Ceylon to Singapore to Malaysia to Indonesia, again to Singapore, then to Australia and New Zealand and finally to Hawaii! Eight one-nighters later, he would celebrate his seventy-third (and next-to-last) birthday one day late at Newark's Symphony Hall, greeted by two thousand school children. Is there any other composer-performer in history who kept such a schedule? Is it any wonder that the program he presented at the Whitney was off-the-cuff rather than carefully planned? The wonder is how effective it was, how effervescently the fabled Ellington charm flowed that night. . . .[14]

That night Togo's ambassador to the United States presented Ellington with a block of the African country's stamps honoring him—along with Bach, Beethoven, and Debussy.[15]

The Duke Ellington Orchestra was on the road again the next day, following a zigzag route up and down the East Coast. With few exceptions, Ellington was playing for ordinary folks in ordinary settings: municipal auditoriums and venues such as the Covered Tree Inn, Timbers Restaurant, Yorktowne Motor Inn. But wherever he went, he conveyed a warm regard for his audiences and unstintingly poured out on them the communal music and personal mystique that by now had blessed virtually the whole world.

The unifying force of Ellington's genius became even more evident in these last years of Ellington's career. Impressions from his foreign travel were incorporated into Ellington's compositions, notably *The Far East Suite*, *The Latin American Suite* and *The*

Ellington's trophy and award room, 1971. (Courtesy Dance Collection, Yale Music Library)

The famous Duke Ellington Orchestra reed section. (Courtesy of Dr. Theodore Shell)

Queen's Suite. Although he didn't try to imitate the various forms of world music, both sights and sounds of other lands and cultures stimulated his creative imagination.

Similarly, he was not hesitant to engage in musical collaboration with a new generation of jazz musicians such as tenor saxophonist John Coltrane and drummer Max Roach. In these matches the old champion is no less daring than the challengers. As Ellington lived out the final decade of his life, some compromises were made for the sake of the band's survival, but it still endured. Ellington had earned the honors bestowed on him. He was no longer young, even though he resisted any reminders of his age. He had seen the deaths of his parents, great soloists such as Blanton and Hodges, Arthur Whetsol, his estranged wife, the irreplaceable Billy Strayhorn, and national heroes such as Franklin Roosevelt, John Kennedy, Robert Kennedy, and Martin Luther King, Jr. Yet the scope of his vision grew larger rather than smaller. Simple Sunday school lessons about a God who created all things and all peoples found mature expression in Ellington's roles as "God's messenger boy" and ambassador-at-large to the world.

Moreover, in programs such as he played at the Whitney, the interweaving of Ellington's compositions—those labeled sacred and those not—suggests that, for Ellington, virtually all his work was dedicated to one end: a celebration of life and the one who created it. His music upended things, destroyed categories, broke up notions of the norm. In the whole range of Ellington's work, wrote Mark Harvey, ". . . there was a transformative process at work, taking what some heard only as popular idioms and recasting or reshaping them as part of a quest for a music that would point toward more transcendent themes."[16] This was art as the theologian Paul Tillich conceived it.

9

God's Messenger

All slang is metaphor, and all metaphor is poetry.
—*G. K. Chesterton*

WHEN DUKE ELLINGTON SPOKE of the Sacred Concert presented at Grace Cathedral in 1965 as an exceptional opportunity, he was thinking about only one event. But that concert led to many other similar ones, and—perhaps more importantly—gave Ellington a new sphere of creativity and self-expression while modifying his own sense of vocation. He described his new self-concept in simple terms. "I like to think of myself as a messenger," he said, and the message was "not directed to God, but to the people."[1] Sometimes the Maestro even called himself "God's messenger boy," which he could not have done without some irony.

The message Duke wanted to deliver consisted of his own beliefs about God, which were rooted in Christian doctrine but idiosyncratically selected and interpreted. The medium was his music, often paired with lyrics of his own making, and enhanced by dance and narrative. And it was *his* music—and his musicians, who employed the range of sounds at their command. The methods used were similar to those he employed in other creative activity. He collaborated. He was attentive to individual gifts and allowed for improvisation. Within his encompassing

THE CATHEDRAL CHURCH  OF ST. JOHN THE DIVINE

By invitation of the Bishop of New York

DUKE ELLINGTON AND HIS ORCHESTRA

PRESENT

A SACRED CONCERT

FRIDAY, JANUARY 19, 1968

8:15 P.M.

THEY WILL BE ASSISTED BY:

ALEC WYTON, ORGANIST AND MASTER OF
CHORISTERS OF THE CATHEDRAL CHURCH

AND

THE CHOIR OF MOTHER A. M. E. ZION CHURCH
Solomon Herriot, Jr., *Director*

THE CHOIRS OF ST. HILDA'S AND ST. HUGH'S SCHOOL
William Toole, *Director*

THE MEN OF THE CATHEDRAL CHOIR

Program for Second Sacred Concert.
(Archives, Cathedral Church of St. John the Divine)

vision and meditative creative process, many different elements were brought together, modified, and transformed into something original and new.

Although each concert was different, the three shared certain characteristics. In all of them styles ranged from low-down blues to ethereal vocalese, and from discordant instrumental orchestrations to simple vocal melodies. Church choirs and professional soloists sang, dancers swayed and stomped, and speakers declaimed. In Ellington's lyrics, the language ranged from poetic paraphrases of Scripture to streetwise slang. These contrasting voices were sometimes used side by side, as when a stern and serious vocal proclamation such as "In the Beginning God" ended with the vernacular double negative "no nothin'" and a spoken recitative made allusions to contemporary life, from television commercials to the space program's Gemini V.

These performances were concerts, not liturgies—and certainly not "jazz masses," as Ellington had to explain repeatedly. But the original concerts were conceived for performance in sacred spaces. These settings themselves helped define the meaning of these events and their impact on performers and audiences, too. (Some of the more than one hundred sacred concert performances, however, did take place outside of a sanctuary or temple setting.) Ellington called the Sacred Concerts a "form of worship."[2] The concerts were an offering to God. They contained elements of worship: prayer, musical "fire-and-brimstone sermonettes," and other expositions of scripture. The "audience" was like a congregation freed to participate by bobbing heads, tapping toes, snapping fingers. People laughed at Ellington's humor, even when it was contrived, and applauded his music enthusiastically. At one college performance shortly before his seventieth birthday, Duke himself led the way, with his clapping hands moving in double arcs to the beat of the boisterous, joyful finale of "Praise God and Dance." This setting of Psalm 150 prompted exuberant response, and Ellington was clearly delighted when people followed the movements of the principal performers with their own "hand-dancing." Duke began encouraging this practice because, he said, it seemed so "worshipfully committed."[3] At the Church of Santa Maria del Mar in Barcelona, people began moving and then finally burst into the aisles to join the professional dancers.

Ellington directed and presided—even if representatives of the hosting church offered an opening prayer or welcoming statement—and he introduced or acknowledged members of the band, or other soloists, as he would in any other venue. But both the soloists and Ellington himself were aware of the significance of the setting. While playing "Come Sunday," Johnny Hodges would roll his eyes upward, as if his sight could penetrate the sanctuary and rise to the vault of heaven. Esther Marrow was close to tears as she sang "Come Sunday," a prayer asking the "Lord of Love" to see her people through. Jon Hendricks scatted with all the joyful abandon of those disciples who were accused of drinking too much wine when the Spirit inspired ecstatic utterances in unknown tongues.

If the concerts can be understood as worship, then Ellington is clearly the worship leader. How one approached or addressed God was a question Ellington continued to ask. When it came to these concerts, however, he preferred to draw from his own religious and musical heritage. He never wrote the jazz mass commissioned by Father Norman O'Connor, and he ignored one cleric's suggestions that he adapt certain elements of the Episcopal service. Ellington didn't like to "jazz up" traditional hymns or represent a specific church tradition. His clarity of purpose in this respect had a powerful effect on the character of these presentations. He and the members of the band—predominantly African American—were not present as tolerantly accepted guests of the prestigious churches where the concerts often were given. They were there to speak a word, to serve as God's messengers, and to give something valuable to all who were present. Ellington's leadership assured that this was their role, despite any anxieties about their offering being rejected. After all, many people thought then—and now—that jazz didn't belong in the church. Ellington bassist Aaron Bell recalled an old Webster's dictionary definition of jazz: "a low type of music that brings out the worst emotions of mankind"—and, in parentheses, "jigaboo music."4

By leading these events, Ellington was adding some new roles to the many he already had. He was "Harlem Renaissance piano tickler; bandleading king of the Cotton Club; romantic composer of sensuous ballads; orchestrator of moods of swing which catapulted jitter-hoppers to manic frenzy; sonic painter of lush soundscapes; transcendent artist; African American cultural icon; world citizen. And on top of that jali, muezzin, cantor, mwalimu, kapelmeister, ecumenist and deacon," wrote Jay Hoggard, a jazz vibraphonist and music faculty member at Wesleyan University.5 Hoggard decided on his musical career at age twelve, after attending a performance of the Second Sacred Concert with his father, A.M.E. Zion Bishop J. Clinton Hoggard. The event was presented April 23, 1967, at the Mother A.M.E. Zion Church in Harlem, prior to its commissioned premiere at St. John the Divine the following January. The juxtaposition of the church's location with nearby jazz clubs was especially powerful. The experience was an epiphany for a young boy witnessing this great jazz band playing in his church: this was jazz and it was also "God's music."

The Sacred Concerts were not attempts to imitate the grand masters of traditional sacred music—oratorios, masses, musical settings of the Passion story. Why would Ellington attempt to write such works when he didn't want to follow the conventions of composing a symphony? The musical elements of call-and-response, blue notes, riffs, improvisation, the twelve- and sixteen-bar blues forms, and thirty-two-bar ballad structure were Ellington's compositional building blocks. So he did not ask his sidemen to adapt their playing to some notion of "sacred music" in the European tradition; nor did he do that himself. The members of the Ellington orchestra performed in their own inimitable style, with the same boldness and verve that characterized night-club appearances. Ellington also incorporated choral harmonies and certain echoes of church music into his concert programs.

The presence of church choirs singing his music and traditional spirituals was significant. In the Sacred Concerts Ellington reunited the strains of black music that had been divided into two types labeled sacred and secular: the spirituals and hymns reserved for Sunday morning, the blues and jazz associated with Saturday night. What he did was to reclaim the sacred origins of jazz and demonstrate that all musical instruments could be employed in praise of God, just as Psalm 150 commanded. In "Praise God and Dance" in the Second Sacred Concert, Ellington didn't simply exhort hearers to praise God; with horns and drums and cymbals played by master musicians, with choirs, vocal soloists, and joyful dancers, he showed just how it could be done.

The element of theatricality in the Sacred Concerts was powerful. This element, combined with the jazz style and uncompromised expression of the orchestra, has prompted Gary Giddins, among others, to characterize Ellington's effort as bringing the Cotton Club revue to the pulpit.[6] But the theatricality of the Sacred Concerts may have more in common with the dramatic elements of worship and church pageantry than with those of the nightclub. Compare the Sacred Concerts, for example, to the medieval cycle plays. Both were set in a cosmic framework, from primordial chaos to creation ("In the Beginning") to a new creation at the end of time ("New World A-Comin'"). Both brought together the community and blurred distinctions between sacred and secular. In the cycle plays, townspeople enacted sacred stories while retaining their own peculiar identities as tanners or tinsmiths, seamstresses or bakers. Ellington kept this human touch with references to contemporary events and with lyrics that drew metaphors from poker and popular entertainment. He involved nonprofessionals, including a child to recite "The Sonnet of the Apple" in "Supreme Being." A contemporary debate ignited by the book *Radical Theology and the Death of God* was alluded to in the recited portions of "Something 'Bout Believing."

Another church influence can be found in Duke's use of the piano in the Sacred Concerts. He characteristically cued performances with a kind of "noodling" at the keyboard—to cue his players, sometimes to get them onto the stage, to feed them melodic ideas, and to create a rhythmic base for the orchestra. In the Sacred Concerts, piano interludes linked different segments of an extended piece and smoothed transitions when there were changes of tempo and mood. And in a sanctuary the similarity between Duke's techniques and those of the church organist or piano player became more apparent. Especially in the "free" churches; the accompanist supports and partly directs the whole service by such practices as playing quietly beneath spoken prayers, setting up sung responses, extending the hymn-singing with a repeated verse or refrain, playing "walking music" for an altar call or the offering. The congregation stands, sits, sings, says "Amen" as prompted by the music. The pianist, who has already begun to move toward the piano bench in anticipation of the preacher's closing phrase, punctuates the end of the sermon. The musician must be attentive and attuned to whatever is happening with the congregation and the other worship leaders, so that the actions, attitude, and moods can be appropriately supported, or modified.

In Ellington's conducting from the piano on stage—and in the sanctuary—can be seen a sophisticated, personalized expansion of such masterful musicianship as he might have observed at church in his early years. Duke's tribute to such church musicians may also be heard in the Second Sacred Concert, when he chose to use an electric piano, probably to imitate the effect of the church organ. Even when the sacred concert program was presented under his direction, Ellington often would include a selection played by the local church organist. In each concert Duke offered at least one piano solo with a theme suggested either by its title ("Meditation" and "The Lord's Prayer") or by program notes ("New World A-Comin'"). These solos may not have been derived from his church tradition so much as from memories of his mother's piano playing.

One helpful approach to assessing the Sacred Concerts is to look at them as a "work in progress," both musically and theologically. Ellington's work in the Sacred Concerts was a process that involved the integration of his faith as it developed—from earliest childhood to the facing of his mortality. This does not mean it was simply his age and the fear of God's judgments that prompted his effort. But the process of writing and performing this music was like a meditative exercise through which he could achieve greater consciousness about his own spirit in relation to the God he worshiped and to the world. Ellington was always open to the spiritual dimension—and it was a key element in his genius; that is one reason why his instrumental music, from the earliest days, touched people so profoundly and created transcendent experience for his listeners.

When Ellington started to express his beliefs self-consciously in words, he used all the language of his experience, from the naïvely literal messages of Sunday school to echoes of sublimely metaphorical scripture. Musically he drew from the heritage of his people. This included the cadences of black preaching and congregational responses; gospel music as well as the more sedate traditions of the churches of Ellington's childhood; the Victorian art songs his mother played; dancing and drumming evolved from early slave festivals; and the chanting or recitative from pageants and dramas witnessed as a youth.

Ellington, exercising his typical collaborative style, also drew inspiration from an expanded cast of players in the Sacred Concerts. Dean Julian Bartlett of Grace Cathedral contributed a poem, which was set to music, titled "A Christmas Surprise," and sung by Lena Horne in A Concert of Sacred Music at the Fifth Avenue Presbyterian Church on December 26, 1965. Maria Dance, the daughter of Stanley and Helen Dance, was credited with suggesting Psalm 150 as a theme. Canon Harold Weicker of St. John the Divine contributed a verse to "Don't Get Down on Your Knees to Pray Until You Have Forgiven Everyone." Ellington incorporated a poetic musing written by Father Gerald Pocock of Montreal, Canada, into the extended piece "Every Man Prays in His Own Language," a central feature of the Third Sacred Concert. In the same thematic piece, Ellington included Roscoe Gill's "Wordless Prayer." A card from the Benedictine Abbey of Regina Laudis in Bethlehem, Connecticut, inspired "Is God a Three-Letter Word for Love?"

Among the professional musicians, Alice Babs stands out as a personified muse for some of Ellington's most beautifully lyric sacred compositions, including "Heaven," "T.G.T.T.," "Almighty God Has Those Angels," and "My Love." Alice, Duke said, imposed no limitations on his composing, so that he could just "write his heart out."[7] She could sing anything and read it flawlessly at sight. What is more, she appreciated and understood Ellington's intentions and added her own warmth and religious feeling to whatever she sang. When Ellington asked her to sing in the Second Sacred Concert, she told him to forget about any salary, just to cover her expenses. Duke said that Alice looked "like an angel" as well as sang like one.[8] Perhaps she embodied that combination of beauty and piety he attributed to his mother.

Yet another participant was intentionally invoked in these settings. Any performance by the orchestra had the capacity to unite people through the music. This dynamic occurred within the band itself, when even men who weren't speaking to each other became linked through their music-making. This unifying power of Ellington's music in performance was further enhanced in sacred settings and with religious texts that acknowledged the "hosts of heaven" to be part of the gathering. In that presence, hearers and performers witness each other being affected by this awareness of a human-divine relationship.

Barry Ulanov described what this was like at St. John the Divine for the premiere of the Second Sacred Concert: "Here were all these people, so many of them were crowded into the place. God knows what the motivation was, from person to person and group to group. But you could feel, very early on, that they hit something they had never expected to hit. It just really caught them, and [they were] very deeply moved by it. And, as always happens, it works two ways. Duke was caught by their being caught. . . . I don't know where I was, but it was enough of a distance so that I didn't have to worry about his meeting my eye or anybody seeing—I could look at him sort of privately. And I saw that he was moved. He was really moved. And it's in the playing."

Performance of Second Sacred Concert at National Presbyterian Church in Washington, D.C. (Courtesy Dr. Theodore Shell)

Duke Ellington with the Reverend John Gensel, long-time pastor to jazz musicians in New York City.
(Courtesy Dance Collection, Yale Music Library)

Thomas Whalley, Alice Babs, and Duke with choir members anticipating the performance of Ellington's Second Sacred Concert at St. John the Divine in 1968. (Courtesy Dance Collection, Yale Music Library)

Tired from rehearsals for the Second Sacred Concert. (Courtesy Dance Collection, Yale Music Library)

Music was Ellington's language, and it was through music that he expressed his most intimate feelings and aspirations, including his aspirations of faith. Duke expressed his love for his mother and grief after her death through the composition "Reminiscing in Tempo." Making a tribute album and, especially, playing Billy Strayhorn's "Lotus Blossom" were comparable means through which Ellington mourned his dear friend and collaborator. It seems natural to conclude then, that the Sacred Concerts were more than musical compositions or experiments with a new setting for his nightclub act. The writing and performing of about forty pieces he identified as sacred was a journey of discovery for Ellington. It led him beyond his own times, even beyond his own traditions—and probably past his own expectations.

The first concert was well grounded in Ellington's upbringing. At the Grace Cathedral performance he included his tribute to his family, a warm idealized memory of parents and grandparents, in the piece called "Heritage." "Come Sunday" was a spiritual ballad rooted in the experience of slavery, from which sprang the bittersweet combination of present suffering, and the assurance of a promised comfort and vindication. This piece was complemented by choral presentations of traditional spirituals. (These were not included on released recordings.)

Even Ellington's fascination with "In the Beginning God" resonates with the likelihood of an early Bible memorization assignment—as does the chanting, in order, of all the names of all the books of the Bible in the development of the piece. "David Danced" not only gave Ellington an opportunity to bring tap dancing into the sanctuary; it also reflected his familiarity with biblical stories. In the first concert, the emphasis lies on getting the information down, accepting the doctrines, and living up to prescribed standards of behavior. "Tell Me It's the Truth," is a text that is all affirmation. "Ain't But the One" presents God as the miracle worker, both in creation and in the acts of Jesus. "Will You Be There?" and "Ninety-nine Percent" exhort the hearers to live by the Ten Commandments—or else.

By the Second Concert, the concerns are broader and the religious maturity seems greater. Spontaneous praise of God springs from all the musical instruments, as well as from all creation, as proclaimed in Psalm 150 or "Praise God and Dance." Faith brings freedom for people to become what they already are and to live by "moral freedoms" (instead of commandments). Simultaneously, Ellington joins these understandings of freedom with cries for political freedom being heard about the globe, as people of color threw off the constraints of colonialism abroad and a segregated society at home.

Just as he constantly reinterpreted other pieces, Ellington changed the way the Sacred Concerts and the individual pieces were presented; the premiere performances differ from the recordings, in terms of program order and in other details. One very telling change is found in the Second Sacred Concert. In one portion of the extended piece called "Freedom," Ellington had young choir members individually come up to a microphone and speak the word in seventeen different languages, then Ellington spoke extemporaneously about freedom, closing with the four "moral freedoms"—which he associated with Billy Strayhorn. In the premiere performance, Ellington spoke using first-person pronouns, and both his face and his voice revealed a depth of emotion that was quite touching. [9] In naming the last of the four freedoms, he spoke of freedom from the pride that would "make me feel that I was better than my brother." For the recording, Ellington delivers the four freedoms in a scripted monologue, using third-person pronouns to speak of "a man" who might feel that kind of pride. In the live presentation, such personal involvement in his message would have been felt by the gathering; there is no comparable experience for anyone hearing the recording, even though the idea is the same.

The theme of forgiveness also is articulated in "Father Forgive," based on a Coventry Cathedral prayer, and by "Don't Get Down on Your Knees to Pray Until You Have Forgiven Everyone." The vernacular lyric catalogues a list of specific wrongs that need to be forgiven others before one engages in prayer. Reflective compositions that Ellington was giving more expression to in later years appear in the Second Concert also. "Heaven" and "Almighty God Has Those Angels" point listeners to a realm beyond earthly life— even though Ellington used images from this world to describe the next. Ellington on electric piano and Alice Babs soaring on wordless vocalese in T.G.T.T. (for "Too Good to Title") articulate phrases that never go where expected. Ellington said that he liked to think Jesus Christ "violated conformity" in the same way.

These movements—away from preachments and toward prayer—are even more evident in the Third Sacred Concert. "Praise God and Dance," from the second concert, and "Tell Me It's the Truth," as well as Toney Watkins' calypso style "Lord's Prayer," from the first concert, were included in the live performance of the third. There's also a brief musical "quote" of a melodic phrase from "T.G.T.T." in the long piece "Every Man Prays in His Own Language." The concert opened with Ellington's piano solo interpretation of "The Lord's Prayer," followed immediately by Alice Babs' singing "My Love." The trombone section provided a lush choral underpinning, and Harry Carney beautifully interpreted the melodic theme on baritone saxophone. The words are like the repeated endearments of a lover, but apparently not a human one. In the tradition of Christian erotic mysticism and metaphorical readings of the Song of Songs, "My Love" is like a love poem written for God.

The remainder of the program, which was significantly cut for later release on LP, included "Is God a Three-Letter Word for Love?" and "Somebody Cares." Ellington attempted to demonstrate his message by employing various music styles and devices, but in the Third Sacred Concert, there's only one "fire and brimstone sermonette." "Ain't Nobody Nowhere Nothin' Without God," sung by Toney Watkins, falls into that category.

Although Ellington began his work on the Sacred Concerts with the notion that he was a messenger whose message was directed to the people, nine years later he was addressing God, and those gathered overheard his prayers. He also gave others, such as Alice Babs and Art Baron, the opportunity to offer their distinct voices in prayer. "My Love" and "Every Man Prays in His Own Language" are directly addressing God, the latter being a series of prayers in various musical tongues—from a swinging piece by the orchestra to two other versions of "The Lord's Prayer" sung a cappella by the choir. Alice Babs created her own Swedish version of the prayer, and, for trombonist Art Baron, Ellington wrote another "Lord's Prayer" to be played on recorder.

"The Majesty of God," written for this concert, expresses awe and humility in both music and words. The instrumental section featuring Carney and Duke is full of mystery, with out-of-time melodic and harmonic explorations that suggest the fear experienced in a strange dream or alien setting. The orchestra in this piece comes in with full, lush chords that build to a climax, as if the curtains had been opened on a great stage. The vocal theme sung by Babs stresses the inability of words to describe God's mystery and the inadequacy of human thought to comprehend the nature of God.

Ellington seems to have moved from an understanding of religion as "getting it down right," to a prayerful contemplation of the love and beauty of God. There are early signs of this change found in the pieces "Meditation" and "T.G.T.T." in the Second

Sacred Concert, but the Abbey event revealed it more fully and conveyed an overall mood in keeping with that kind of interiority. Although it is missing in the commercial recording, "Every Man Prays in His Own Language" included a recitative given by Toney Watkins over the choir's humming. The words, quite clearly in Ellington's language, implored: "Forgive us our necessities, and the hunger that makes them necessary." Ellington was too guarded to display in concert his most intimate thoughts and prayers. But looking at the changes expressed in his music, there seems to be a break—a period of silence between the preachiness and exuberance of earlier sacred music—and the prayerful devotion, awe bordering on fear, and longing of later pieces. This suggests a change of perception, perhaps even a revelation, which is being simultaneously experienced and interpreted through the music.

But even the music becomes an inadequate vehicle—as the first two lines in Ellington's prayer suggest. "The words we use are most ordinary. The noise we make is neither serene nor loud enough." However Ellington's music and words are critically judged, the Sacred Concerts are themselves evidence of an encounter between Ellington and the One whom he honored in them. Although he began by assuming the role of a messenger, at the end Ellington may well have been the recipient of God's message.

The significance of the Sacred Concerts may not have been fully understood by Ellington even though he undertook them with all the passion of a mission. "Religious vision" is the term used by Mark S. Harvey to describe what Ellington articulated and embodied in his Sacred Concerts. "Ellington's religious vision was broader than even he could imagine—for in fact he spoke to people of all sorts and conditions, beyond categories of even believers and unbelievers. His faith was grounded in love, and . . . love had to be limitless, unconditional, and full of possibility," wrote Harvey, a musician, educator, and United Methodist minister. "This personal faith undergirded . . . a social ethic of celebration, one which joined ecstatic praise with deep concern for social justice."[10]

Ralph J. Gleason, who arranged for an NET filming of the first concert, attended a regular Ellington concert shortly thereafter and found that program seemed basically religious to him. He wrote, "I doubt that I shall ever hear Ellington play again, in any context, without thinking of it as religious music."[11] The sacred music represented a completion of Ellington's earlier work and was also what Harvey has called a fulfillment of Ellington's religious vision. Writing and performing the three concerts represented a culminating achievement in which Ellington could bring together the widest range of musical elements: his own personal history and the African-American musical heritage, his religious faith—and his hopes for the world and all its people. Hoggard also concluded: "With his Sacred Concerts, Ellington successfully amalgamated the sacred and secular realms of music in an organic, sanctified, totality. . . . For me, this music ranks among the great achievements of the twentieth century."[12]

Several months after the presentation of the Third Sacred Concert, Ellington was playing at the Rainbow Grill, where he was visited by his friend Edmund Anderson, who had come there with his wife on Christmas Eve. The evening before, Ellington had presented that concert again, this time at St. Augustine's Presbyterian Church in the Bronx. The Andersons explained that they had planned to attend midnight mass, but instead came to hear Duke. "We were going to church," Anderson said. And Ellington replied, "You're in church when you're *here*." "He did tell us that he had so much more he wanted to do. This was after the Abbey concert, which was not a very successful concert because he was so ill and he kept walking off the stage. He was very tired. The man was dying then, really." Anderson had not seen his friend since the London performance. He told Duke, "I feel that the concert at the Abbey was very spiritual. Also, the music was more spiritual than the other two concerts were. And [Duke] said, 'I have so much more I want to do. So much more I *have* to do.' Those were his very words."

During the final months of his illness Ellington continued to lead his orchestra. When he finally had to be hospitalized, he received visitors with wit and grace and continued to work on his musical projects. He had his piano installed in his hospital room so that he could play and record his ideas on cassette tapes. *Queenie Pie*, the comic opera he had wanted to do for so long, was one of his projects. He and Edmund Anderson were also working on "Duke Ellington's history of jazz." One day Ellington walked with his friend to the elevator, a long walk for him. Anderson said, "I'm so proud of you, of what you've done since I've known you. My God, it's been forty years. I'm so proud of you." Duke gave him the usual four kisses that he gave everybody, gave Anderson a big smile, he said. Anderson was thinking about the early days of their friendship. He would have to call downstairs to make sure Ellington wasn't sent around to the back door when he came over. Even after Ellington had gained some recognition, if they were going out downtown in the city Anderson would have to call first to be sure his friend would be welcome. "Realize what had happened to this man," he said. "He was received at the Vatican and all over Europe and degrees here and there. He had such an incredible mind, and at this point he was being wined and dined and flattered by everybody. He was all over the world."

Evie Ellis was also diagnosed with cancer, and for some time they could only talk to each other by phone. Ellington wanted to finish a composition called *Three Black Kings*, a three-part suite in honor of Balthazaar, the dark-skinned king legendarily associated with Christ's nativity; King Solomon, and Martin

Luther King, Jr. He and Mercer listened over and over to cassettes of the recording of the Westminster Abbey concert. Duke had planned to do some studio work to supplement the performance material, but at the end he was giving Mercer instructions about how to cut and splice the available material so that it could be released. His eyesight was failing. Scraps of paper written in a large hand became his daily log or journal for recording his thoughts. Mercer found one that read, "I'm easy to please. All I want is to have everyone in the palm of my hand."[13]

All this time Duke failed to make a will, his chosen strategy against the inevitable end of life: If I don't acknowledge that you exist, you have no power over me. Duke Ellington had said that he didn't believe in death. Death was nonexistence. In his song "Ain't Nobody Nowhere Nothin' Without God," Duke revealed how he saw unbelief and nonexistence to be linked. Anyone who doesn't believe in God doesn't exist, the slangy, upbeat song claims in unequivocal terms. So anyone who does believe has to exist. Of course, he had that black bag of remedies with him and his superstitions, all suggesting that he was acutely aware of his mortality. A scrawled poem on a piece of Zurich hotel stationary reveals that Duke was, for some time, on intimate terms with a man facing his own emptiness and death.[14]

His Every Dawn Crackled up
an Empty Day
with promises of only the Blackest
Stormy Night
He Knew the Tides of Hunger
His Ears Racing with the Echos [sic] of
His Own Crying & Pleading
His Spiritual Nakedness Felt
Only the Recoiling Caresses of Insecurity
So Close to Death He Could Smell it.

Michael James remembers a visit with his uncle toward the end. Ellington had been sleeping, and other visitors had left. "When Duke woke up, he pushed up, got to the edge of the bed, sat there," Michael said. "He looked out the window. At that point he hadn't been outside in five or six weeks. He looked out that window at the light, then shook his head, looked toward the window, shook his head again, as if to say, 'I'll never see it again. I can't beat this one.'"

Over his bed Duke had a sign of those two words "God" and "Love," cut-out letters pasted up there in a cross. In mid-May people began receiving Ellington's Christmas cards. They always came late, as late as July. But this year they were not as late, and some people thought he was sending them early. It was a simple card. On a background of brilliant blue were gold letters spelling G O D in a horizontal line; the letters spelling L O V E were placed vertically, with a common O in the middle to form a cross.

James wasn't there the night his uncle died, but Ruth Ellington Boatwright was with her brother for several hours. "He acted out clicking a camera," Michael said, as if to say, "I'm taking a picture of you with me." That night alone with his sister Duke looked at her and said, "Kisses, kisses." "I picked him up, for he was shrunken and light, and kissed him. . . . Then he said, 'More kisses,' and I kissed him some more." Around his neck he was wearing that cross Ruth had given him when she was sixteen. "He always kissed the cross before he flew anywhere. That night he kissed the cross as if to say, 'I'm flying away.'"

Edward Kennedy Ellington died at 3:45 the next morning. Although he was wasted by cancer, the cause of death was pneumonia, the disease that had almost claimed his life some seventy years earlier.

Duke's shoes.
(Photo © Herman Leonard)

10

Coda

DUKE ELLINGTON ALWAYS RESISTED finishing a composition. Frequently the ending of an Ellington piece does not leave us with an expected feeling of resolution and completion, but rather suggests that we are moving on to something that is not yet fully realized—waiting in the wings. The Maestro's closing punctuation was often a musical question mark. Ellington's fascination with trains is a common musical motif that also has the effect of suggesting there's more to come. In "Daybreak Express" and "Happy-Go-Lucky Local," depicting two different kind of train rides, we hear the sounds of a train as it starts up, then moves on, the pitches of a wailing whistle, roaring engines, and clattering wheels altered by the changes in speed and apparent distance from those it passes by. Even as the train slows down and pulls into the station, we know that it will leave again on another journey to some unnamed destination.

A large folder of music lies open on a long wooden table in the research room of the National Museum of American History Archives Center where a professor of music composition is examining the fifteen-part score of an Ellington-Strayhorn piece. The instrumental parts are labeled in Duke's graceful scrawl with the nicknames and names of sidemen in the Ellington Orchestra.

There's "Rabbit" for the inimitable alto saxophonist Johnny Hodges and "Cat" for high-note specialist William Anderson on trumpet, even Harry Carney's name is written on the score—although from the time he joined the band in 1927 no one else regularly played the baritone saxophone for Ellington. Lawrence Brown, Russell Procope, Britt Woodman, Harold Ashby, Quentin Jackson, Sam Woodyard, Aaron Bell, Louie Bellson, Buster Cooper, plunger-mute expert Cootie Williams—they're all there on the countless pages of manuscripts the Smithsonian Institution acquired from the Ellington estate in 1988. For devotees and scholars, the scores render a visual as well as an aural impression of how Duke conceived his music. He heard the specific, characteristic sound, range, and timbre each of his instrumentalists could make, whether they were soaring on an improvised solo or simply blowing the single-note root of a chord while other players filled out the harmony with Ellington's amazing color tones and distinctive chord voicings.

Ellington did not settle on a definitive version of a composition which can be replicated by others now. He reworked old material, expanding, reinterpreting, combining it with other treatments. At the piano he could alter a piece's mood and tempo simply by the introduction he might play on a given night. In the recording studio orchestrations were worked out on the spot, and Ellington's interaction with his sidemen produced effects that cannot be translated into musical notation. He continually interpreted and reinterpreted his own work, which is part of the secret of its enduring appeal.

This constant evolution of Ellington's vision, style, and musical substance constitutes a subject of abiding interest and debate for musicologists and others who want to understand and appropriate Ellington's musical legacy. Those transcribing, performing, and arranging Ellington and his collaborators' music now face many questions and challenges. (His collaborative work with Billy Strayhorn is a unique puzzle because they were so much of one mind. Moreover, it seems that the two of them often conspired to avoid a clear demarcation of their individual contributions.) Ellington, as no other jazzman, combined the improvisatory, performance-oriented character of jazz with compositional genius that shaped distinct musical elements into a cohesive whole. In addition, the effects he achieved were integrally linked to the personalities and musical skills of his players—and to the interactive, sometimes unspoken, communication between and among them.

When Ellington's recordings and scores differ, then what? Does a soloist try to play an improvised solo note for note, or exercise his own gifts for interpretation? The conventions of jazz performance seem to argue against "preservation" of a fixed legacy when it comes to this music. Yet performance is part of the legacy.

Since Ellington's death, a treasure-house of orchestra scores, privately made and unreleased recordings, and personal memorabilia has become available. Hundreds of new compact discs have been released from the private collections and from reissues of commercially recorded material dating back to the 1920s. This collection of Ellington music—scores, recordings, transcriptions, material now catalogued and published—is available for many purposes and will keep jazz repertory orchestras, Ellington fans, discographers, and musicologists well occupied for years.

During the centennial year of Ellington's birth, Duke's contributions have been honored and explored in countless ways both here and abroad. The Pulitzer Prize board awarded a posthumous Special Citation Award that stressed the ways his music embodied principles of democracy and acknowledged the denial of such a prize in 1965. Jazz radio stations devoted whole days to Ellington's recorded music, and still only scratched the surface. Through the year there were documentary radio programs, two public television specials featuring the Lincoln Center Jazz Orchestra with Wynton Marsalis, seminars and performances at universities across the country.

The Lincoln Center Jazz Orchestra and the Smithsonian Jazz Masterworks Orchestra both went on major tours. April issues of *Emerge, Jazziz,* and *American Legacy* were devoted to Ellington, and newspapers carried retrospective features proclaiming him an American original. Major reissues of recordings were put out by RCA Victor and Sony/Columbia. Performances of the sacred music and other commemorative concerts were going on in major cities such as Los Angeles and Washington, D.C. During the winter holiday season, choreographer Donald Byrd and David Berger, composer and conductor, collaborated on a successful national tour of *The Harlem Nutcracker,* a modern dance production based on the Ellington-Strayhorn version of *The Nutcracker Suite. Black, Brown and Beige* was revived as well. Luther Henderson, a former Ellington orchestrator, paired Ellington's music with Shakespeare in *Play On!*

Ellington family members carrying on the Ducal tradition include grandson Paul Ellington, who assumed leadership of the Duke Ellington Orchestra after Mercer died in 1996. Picking up and taking the band to a Bermuda date immediately after his father's funeral, Mercer had conducted the band for twenty-two years. He and his daughter Mercedes, a dancer and choreographer, had both been instrumental in the 1981 production of *Sophisticated Ladies* on Broadway. During the Centennial observances, and even earlier, Mercedes Ellington worked with symphony orchestras across the country to present a program of music, narrative, and dance called *Sophisticated Ellington*. For years Ruth Ellington Boatwright had promoted performances of the Sacred Concert music; this year her son Michael James served in an advisory capacity to Jazz at Lincoln Center's Ellington centennial events.

Ellington is enjoying a renaissance among collegiate and high school jazz bands as well. Jazz at Lincoln Center has made transcriptions in newly published scores available to high schools and colleges. Marsalis's own compositions reflect his debt to Ellington's influence. *Blood on the Fields*, for which Marsalis was awarded the Pulitzer Prize in 1997, owes much to Ellington's conceptualization of musical narrative, as in *Black, Brown and Beige*. Among those schools with long histories of offering courses on Ellington are U.C.L.A., where jazz guitarist Kenny Burrell teaches the class, and Berklee College of Music, where Ellington's compositional techniques are taught. On April 29, 1999, the musical world came close to following the late Miles Davis's proposal that all musicians should get together on one day and get down on their knees and thank Duke Ellington.

If Ellington's musical creativity still lacks widespread recognition, other aspects of his personal legacy are waiting to be discovered or fully appreciated. While a professor of composition was copying Ellington manuscripts at the Archives Center, an African-American professor of philosophy and religious studies was investigating Ellington's involvement with the movie *Paris Blues*. A graduate student in American history was working on a doctoral dissertation that examines Ellington's interaction with major social and political figures and issues, including the Cold War and the civil rights struggle. Someone else was photocopying his extended personal correspondence with Ellington; another, examining Ellington's religious books and devotional material. The National Museum of American History, which

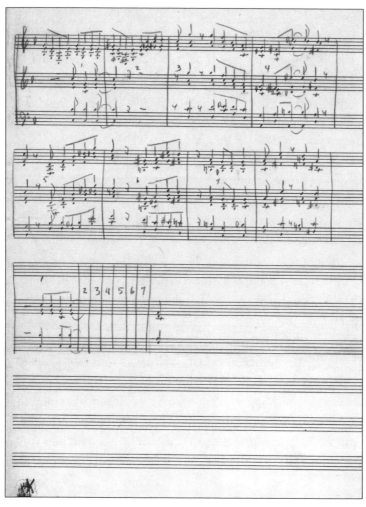

Original manuscript in Duke's handwriting.
(Courtesy Duke Ellington Collection, Archives Center, NMAH)

houses the Archives Center, is also the site of an annual presentation by students at the Duke Ellington School for the Arts, where young musicians and other artists seek disciplined expression of their own unique talents and personalities, thus honoring Ellington's artistic ethic in the most faithful way.

Ellington's sacred music was presented in concert by the Smithsonian Jazz Masterworks Orchestra at the National Cathedral in Washington, D.C., on the centennial anniversary of his birthday. Singers in the Morgan State University Choir were obviously fully engaged in the music, their faces aglow and smiling, their bodies moving subtly with the rhythm. They "swung" Duke's lightweight lyrics on "Something 'Bout Believing " better than did the church choirs Ellington included in his Sacred Concerts. When a more serious mood was required, these young men and women seemed musically and spiritually in complete harmony with soprano Devonne Gardner—one of Ellington's original soloists—and the orchestra in a beautifully nuanced interpretation of "Is God a Three-Letter Word for Love?"

Though he said no one could ever teach him anything, throughout his career Ellington encouraged students and the music educators making a place for jazz in the nation's colleges and schools. Part of the Ellington legacy is a model for creativity and performance that stresses freedom and innovation, enhancement of individual gifts, and unique selfhood.

"No one else can do it the way you can," was the message he communicated to his instrumentalists and singers, and they exceeded their own expectations. "He had a way of looking right through you and pulling something out of you that you didn't even know you had," said Sathima Bea Benjamin, a native of South Africa who made some recordings with Ellington in Paris in the mid 1960s, only recently rediscovered. She is now performing and recording from a New York base. "He still colors my path," she said as she spoke of feeling that his spirit was involved in her reclaiming what he gave her years ago. The sentiments she expressed are not unusual. The people whose lives were touched by Duke Ellington say he gave them more than his music. And they speak of him as if they expected him to walk in from the next room, not as someone who has been gone for twenty-five years.

When Ellington was dying, he asked his friend June Norton to come see him. She knew it would be the last opportunity to speak with him, and she wanted somehow to acknowledge not only their friendship, but also the larger meaning of his life. She hadn't thought out the words ahead of time, but when the moment came they were there. "You know, Duke, most of us—mankind—walk the surface of the earth. But you have thrust your feet deep into the soil and planted seeds that have borne fruit and will continue to bear fruit and continue to inspire people and to nourish them all their lives." Then Ellington's jaw just dropped, she said. "He sat there and he looked at me and he took my hands, and he held them together between his without saying a word." Duke told her he wanted to autograph his book for her. Honoring his request to come back for it later that night, she waited outside while it took Ellington an hour or more to write his inscription in that book. "You could see the pain in his signature," she said. "He wrote it in French."

Duke once was engaged in conversation with a stranger on a train, a refugee who had played chamber music and was asking Duke about his approach to music. Ellington said, "I'm something like a farmer. A farmer that grows things. He plants his seeds and I plant mine. He has to wait until spring to see his come up, but I can see mine right after I plant it. That night. I don't have to wait."[1]

Ellington did get to see some of the seeds he planted come up and bloom in the dark that very night. But others are waiting for the late rains. The soil that Ellington thrust his feet into deeply was life itself—the history of his people, his family, the music of many cultures, the sights and sounds and smells around him, the religious heritage he grew up with and the contemporary voices speaking about God in his adulthood. Perhaps most of all, he plumbed the recesses of his own mind, heart, and soul. In his autobiography Ellington wrote about the human need for self-disclosure and acceptance, opposed by the fear of rejection. Ann K. Kuebler, a Smithsonian archivist, has suggested that the personal artifacts he left behind (the private correspondence, the poetry scribbled on hotel stationary, deathbed notes and ruminations) convince her that Ellington, for all his guardedness and emotional privacy (one of his most striking personal characteristics), wanted to be known and understood—not as the Cotton Club entertainer, the suave, sophisticated man of the world, the consummate composer, the sun amidst several orbits of persons devoted to him professionally and personally—but as a human being, complex and magnificent, but also flawed, who gave himself completely to the life and vocation he believed was uniquely his. Such a man could reveal God to us, and us to ourselves.

Ellington embodied and ennobled the conflicts and the achievements of his age. Even his character flaws and inner contradictions are magnifications of the struggles of his contemporaries and their descendants. He gave us a magnificently human example of one striving to transcend these conflicts while simultaneously giving of himself to the world.

In Ellington's collection of devotional reading there was a Wisconsin church bulletin for Palm Sunday 1971. On the back was a brief message, which had been underlined in several places. Reading the whole sentences containing the underlined passages comes out like this: "To believe in the providence of God means to be anchored in those realities which are timeless. . . . Rather than being an optimist or a pessimist, the man of faith is a realist, a man with strength to look at the changing world and see God at work bringing renewal and healing in the midst of decay and suffering." And then, by themselves, were the words: "they could sing."

Duke Ellington has been blithely called a cultural icon. The word 'icon,' in its original sense, refers to a prayerfully created and dedicated work of art, a picture or an image through which the divine nature or word can be mediated to the viewer. As such, the image is no longer a lifeless object, but one animated by a living spirit. In this sense, Ellington is an icon. And his music is sacramental, too; because it is also a mediator of life-giving spirit. His art unveils the glory of what is luminously holy, but hidden, in the material world and in human flesh.

Ellington's single-minded dedication to music was as passionate as any saint's devotion to personal holiness. Colored by the context of his life and times, Duke's genius was shaped by a disciplined capacity for attention and reflection. He saw value and uniqueness where others saw only the ordinary and prosaic. His great passion and work sprang from an awareness of the presence of God in all of life. The immense legacy of Edward Kennedy Ellington, his art and his witness, is entrusted to future generations to appropriate for their own enrichment and blessing.

ACKNOWLEDGEMENTS

Those who know of my fascination with Duke Ellington will not be surprised to see this book, but I am. Largely because of the vision of Gwendolin Herder, president and publisher of Crossroad, and the persistent guidance of my editor, Barbara Leah Ellis, my interest in Ellington's sacred music has been turned into a biographical work. This book would not have been written without their help and the early encouragement of Penelope Duckworth and Joan Ohanneson.

I wish to thank persons associated with Yale University when this interest was first explored: Peter Hawkins, Harry Adams, Victoria Sirota, Frank Tirro, Willie Ruff, Vivian Perlis, Jerry Streets, Ken Crilly, Suzanne Eggleston, Janet Gordon, Joanna Weber, and Vincent and Martha Oneppo. I am also indebted to the Yale University Music Library for photographs reprinted in this volume.

As a fellow in the 1998 Coolidge Colloquium sponsored by the Association for Religion and Intellectual Life, I was able to do research and interviews in New York City while being inspired and encouraged by colloquium participants. Research assistance was generously given by Michael Lampen, Grace Cathedral archivist; Wayne Kempton, archivist at the Cathedral Church of St. John the Divine; and George E. Boziwick of the New York Public Library for the Performing Arts. Reuben Jackson and Ann

Kuebler of the Archives Center, National Museum of American History, provided professional assistance and personal insights. Dave Burgevin, also of the NMAH staff, was most helpful with photographs. And I am especially grateful to John Edward Hasse for his discography. My debt to his and Mark Tucker's scholarship will be evident to those familiar with their work. Barry Ulanov's biography was also a significant source of insight.

David Hajdu, Krin Gabbard, Jeff Friedman, Charles Waters, Jr., John Schweizer, Sjef Hoefsmit, Theodore Hudson, Ann Kuebler, and Joyce Apsel read portions of the manuscript in its early stages and helped me refine the text, for which none of them should be held responsible. Others who made valuable contributions are Loren Schoenberg, Art Baron, David Berger, Phil Schaap, Walter Schaap, Peter Townsend, Mark Harvey, Morris Hodara, Mac Grimmer, Lisa Barg, and Brooks Kerr. Richard Ehrenzeller shared rare recordings, and Earl Okin provided programs from Ellington's 1933 European tour. Dr. Theodore A. Shell made available his personal photographs. Jim Luce, Kim Childs, Lisa Hamilton, and Phil Mattson worked with me on other Ellington projects, and *The Christian Century* and *Christianity and the Arts* published related articles. The Reverend John Gensel, the Reverend John Yaryan, and Gordon Ewing, now deceased, provided me with valuable information. Over several years, I interviewed many persons who are not named here, but whose insights I am grateful for.

Finally I thank Roger Vicker for computer expertise; Lucille and Allen Hutchinson, Kevan and Dawn Hitch, and Jack and Shirley Miller for East Coast hospitality; Karen Johnson and Elaine Neeley, who were there when needed with just what was needed. Other friends, ministerial colleagues, and my family, whose loving support I relied on, have my enduring gratitude.

CHRONOLOGY

Note to reader: Events of Duke Ellington's life appear on the left-hand side pages, and corresponding world events appear on the right-hand side pages.

1899 Birth of Edward Kennedy Ellington

1913 Writes "Soda Fountain Rag"

1915 Birth of Ruth Ellington, sister
1917 Wins scholarship to Pratt Institute
      Forms Duke's Serenaders
1918 Marries Edna Thompson

1919 Birth of son, Mercer
1923 Moves to New York with musician friends
1923 The Washingtonians begin playing various New York
      clubs

1926 Forms business partnership with Irving Mills
      "Black and Tan Fantasy"
1927 Cotton Club engagement
      Harry Carney joins band
1928 Johnny Hodges joins band
1929 Separates from Edna Thompson
      Black and Tan film
1930 "Mood Indigo"
1931 Leaves Cotton Club

1933 Tours England and France
1935 Daisy Kennedy Ellington (mother) dies
      Symphony in Black film, "Reminiscing in Tempo"
1937 James Edward Ellington (father) dies
1939 Billy Strayhorn joins band as arranger and lyricist
      Break with Irving Mills, second European tour
      Blanton-Webster Years
1940 Signs with RCA Victor
1941 *Jump for Joy* "Take the 'A' Train"
1942 Founds Tempo Music
1943 Carnegie Hall premiere
      Black, Brown and Beige

1899 Publication of *The Interpretation of Dreams* by Freud
1912 Woodrow Wilson elected president

1914 World War I begins

1917 United States enters war
      First jazz recording
1918 Race riots in twenty-five cities, eighty-three lynchings
      End of World War I
1919 Prohibition begins

1925 Massive rally of the Ku Klux Klan in Washington, D.C.

1929 Stock Market crash

1932 Franklin D. Roosevelt elected president
1933 Prohibition repealed

1941 United States enters World War II

1947 *The Liberian Suite*

1953 "Satin Doll" and *Piano Reflections*

1956 Newport Jazz Festival Sensation
Columbia Records

1963 *My People*
State Department Tour

1965 *Impressions of the Far East*
1965 *A Concert of Sacred Music*
1967 Death of Billy Strayhorn
1968 *Second Sacred Concert*

1969 Seventieth Birthday Party at the White House
1971 University of Wisconsin
Tour of Soviet Union

1973 Third Sacred Concert and last European tour
Music Is My Mistress
1974 Ellington dies May 24

1945 Atomic bombs dropped on Japan
End of World War II

1950 Korean Conflict begins
1953 Korean Conflict ends
1954 Segregated public schools declared unconstitutional

1960 John F. Kennedy elected president

1963 President Kennedy assassinated
Civil Rights March on Washington
1964 Passage of Civil Rights bill
Gulf of Tonkin resolution

1968 Martin Luther King, Jr., and Robert Kennedy
assassinated
Richard M. Nixon elected president
1969 U.S. invades Cambodia in Vietnam War

1972 President Nixon elected to a second term
1973 Vietnam peace agreement signed

NOTES

CHAPTER 1: RECAPITULATION

1. Cooke, "The Duke," in *Fun & Games with Alistair Cooke*, p. 201.

2. Jeff Friedman, "An Appreciation of Duke," *Berklee Today*, Vol. 10, No. 3 (Spring 1999), p. 22.

3. Dance, *The World of Duke Ellington*, p. 2.

4. Dance, quoted by Mercer Ellington, with Stanley Dance, *Duke Ellington in Person, An Intimate Memoir.* (Boston: Houghton Mifflin Company, 1978), p. 218.

5. June Norton, interview by author, May 24, 1999.

6. Tape of The Duke Ellington Society (TDES, Inc.) meeting with Herb Martin, Henry Miller, and Joya Sherrill, September 21, 1994, courtesy of TDES, Inc., and Morris Hodara.

7. Material for this description of Ellington's funeral was drawn from several sources: "Stanley Dance: The Funeral Address," with a descriptive preface by editor Sinclair Traill, *Jazz Journal* 27/7 (July 1974), pp. 14–15, as reprinted in Mark Tucker, editor, *The Duke Ellington Reader.* (New York: Oxford University Press, 1993), pp. 381–384; CBS-TV film from the funeral service; Alice Babs, "My Memories of Duke," from Ellington '94 International Conference program, Stockholm, Sweden; interviews with June Norton, Brooks Kerr, Mark S. Harvey, and Edmund Anderson.

CHAPTER 2: THE ROAD TAKEN

1. Tape of graduation speeches and reception courtesy Jeff Friedman, associate professor of jazz composition, Berklee College of Music.
2. Richard O. Boyer, "The Hot Bach—III," *The New Yorker*, July 8, 1944; reprinted in *The Duke Ellington Reader*, p. 244.
3. Lambert, *Duke Ellington: A Listener's Guide*, p. 31.
4. Ellington, *Music Is My Mistress*, p. 452.
5. Barry Ulanov, interview by author, Oct. 21, 1998.
6. Jon Hendricks, Sacred Music segment, Duke Ellington Centennial Radio Project, Lucegroup and Public Radio International, aired in 1999.
7. Courtesy Mac Grimmer, member of The Duke Ellington Society, Washington, D.C., chapter.
8. *A Duke Named Ellington, Part II*, produced by Terry Carter; written by Leonard Malone, the American Masters series, Council for Positive Images, Inc., Santa Monica, 1988.
9. Ellington, *Music Is My Mistress*, p. 260.
10. Ulanov interview.
11. R.D. Darrell, "Black Beauty," *disques* (Philadelphia: H. Royer Smith, June 1932), reprinted in *The Duke Ellington Reader*, p. 64.
12. Ruth Ellington Boatwright, interview by author, Jan. 7, 1993.
13. *The Duke Ellington Centennial Edition*, The Complete RCA-Victor Recordings (1927–1973), RCA Victor/BMG Classics, 1999.

CHAPTER 3: WASHINGTON DAYS

1. Ellington, *Music Is My Mistress*, pp. 12–15.
2. Mac Grimmer.
3. Annetta Rhea Smith, interview, May 2, 1999.

CHAPTER 4: HARLEM AND HOLLYWOOD

1. Frank A. Salamone, "The Sacred Element in Ellington's Music: From the Cotton Club to the Cathedral," *Jazz and American Culture*, a Web-journal.

2. Roger Pryor Dodge, in Hot Records Society's *H.R.S. Rag* October 15, 1940, reprinted in *The Duke Ellington Reader*, p. 456.

3. For musical analysis see Tucker, *Ellington: The Early Years*, pp. 242–248.

4. For an example of this in film, see Gabbard, *Jammin' at the Margins: Jazz and the American Cinema*, pp. 177–184.

5. Gabbard, *Jammin' at the Margins: Jazz and the American Cinema*, pp. 161–167, and *Jazz Cocktails*, by Kino Video, 1997.

6. Irving Mills, "I Split with Duke When Music Began Side-tracking," in *Down Beat*, Ellington Silver Jubilee issue, November 5, 1952, reprinted in *The Duke Ellington Reader*, p. 274.

CHAPTER 5: LOST AND FOUND

1. Ulanov, *Duke Ellington*, p. 201.

2. Ellington, *Music Is My Mistress*, p. 86.

3. Ulanov, *Duke Ellington*, p. 165.

4. Edmund Anderson, interview by author, October 22, 1998.

5. Brooks Kerr, interview by author, August 4, 1998.

6. Edward Morrow, "Duke Ellington on Gershwin's 'Porgy,'" *New Theatre*, December 1935, reprinted in *The Duke Ellington Reader*, pp. 116–117.

7. Hajdu, *Lush Life: A Biography of Billy Strayhorn*, pp. 53–58.

8. Friedman, "An Appreciation of Duke," p. 23.

9. Ellington, *Music Is My Mistress*, p. 156.

Chapter 6: Dreams and Realities

1. Friedman, "An Appreciation of Duke," p. 22.

2. Peter Townsend, "Ellington '42, A Year in the Life," paper presented at Ellington '99, May 1, 1999.

3. Gabbard, *Jamming' at the Margins: Jazz and the American Cinema*, pp. 177–184.

4. *Blue Melodies*, Kino Video, New York, 1997.

5. Ulanov, *Duke Ellington*, pp. 206–207.

6. Hasse, liner notes for *Beyond Category: The Musical Genius of Duke Ellington*, produced by Smithsonian Recordings and BMG.

7. Program notes, *A Concert of Sacred Music by Duke Ellington*, Grace Cathedral, San Francisco, Sept. 16, 1965, courtesy Cathedral Archives.

8. Alexandre Rado, interview by author, May 24, 1995.

Chapter 7: Rebirth, Rejection, and Sweet Revenge

1. Charles H. Waters, Jr., "Anatomy of a Cover: The Story of Duke Ellington's Appearance on the Cover of *Time* Magazine," *Annual Review of Jazz Studies*, Vol. 6, 1993, pp. 1–64.

2. Archives Center, National Museum of American History, Smithsonian Institution. Also appears in Waters' article.

3. Don George, *Sweet Man* (New York: G.P. Putnam's Sons, 1981), pp. 117–120.

4. Waters, "Anatomy of a Cover: The Story of Duke Ellington's Appearance on the Cover of *Time* Magazine," p. 18.

5. Harris, *The Rise of Gospel Blues: The Music of Thomas Andrew Dorsey in the Urban Church*, p. 185.

6. Derek Jewell, *Duke: A Portrait of Duke Ellington*, p. 138, quoted by Andrew Homzy, *"Black, Brown and Beige* in Duke Ellington's Repertoire, 1943–1973," *Black Music Research Journal*, Vol. 13, No. 2, (Fall 1933), p. 96.

7. Irving Townsend "When Duke Records," *Just Jazz 4*, eds. Sinclair Traill and the Hon. Gerald Lascelles (London: Souvenir Press, 1960), pp. 15–21, quoted in *The Duke Ellington Reader*, p. 320.

8. Tucker, *The Duke Ellington Reader*, p. 295.

9. Information courtesy Sjef Hoefsmit of the Duke Ellington Music Society, Inc.

10. Gabbard, *Jamming' at the Margins: Jazz and the American Cinema*, pp. 192–203.

11. John Hohenberg, *The Pulitzer Diaries*, p. 146–47.

12. Pulitzer Prize office.

13. Hohenberg, *The Pulitzer Diaries*, p. 146.

14. Hasse, *Beyond Category: The Life and Genius of Duke Ellington*, p. 356.

15. "Talk of the Town," *The New Yorker*, Aug. 14, 1965, pp. 19–20.

16. Hentoff, reprinted in *The Duke Ellington Reader*, p. 363.

17. Ellison, reprinted in *The Duke Ellington Reader*, p. 398.

CHAPTER 8: WIDER HORIZONS

1. Mark S. Harvey, "New World A-Comin': The Sacred Concerts and Duke Ellington's Religious Vision," paper presented at Ellington '99, April 30, 1999, p. 9.

2. Grace Cathedral Archives.

3. Grace Cathedral Archives, oral history project.

4. Film of panel discussion, Ellington '90, courtesy Charles Waters, Jr.

5. Ellington, *Music Is My Mistress*, p. 261.

6. June Norton, interview by author, May 24, 1999.

7. Ellington, *Music Is My Mistress*, pp. 156–161.

8. Jay Hoggard, interview by author.

9. See Hajdu's biography for a comprehensive treatment of the relationship and its effect on Strayhorn.

10. Program bulletin courtesy of David Berger.

11. Igo/Ewing Itinerary, courtesy of the late Gordon Ewing.

12. From ABC-TV film footage, private collection.

13. Personal interview by author, May 3, 1998, and *New Orleans Times-Picayune*, April 27, 1970.

14. Dan Morgenstern, liner notes, *Duke Ellington Live at the Whitney*, Impulse! IMPD-173, GRP Records, 1995.

15. Igo/Ewing Itinerary.

16. Harvey, " 'New World A-Comin',", p. 9.

CHAPTER 9: GOD'S MESSENGER

1. "Ellington to Perform at Church," Richmond (Calif.) Independent, April 13, 1969.

2. Ibid.

3. Ellington, *Music Is My Mistress*, p. 285.

4. Personal interview by author, July 13, 1998.

5. Hoggard, program notes for his compact disc *Something 'Bout Believing*, and program notes for *Hallelujah!*, performance of Ellington sacred music by the Smithsonian Jazz Masterworks Orchestra, April 29, 1999.

6. Gary Giddins, "At the Pulpit" in *Riding on a Blue Note* (New York: Oxford University Press, 1981), reprinted in *The Duke Ellington Reader*, p. 376.

7. Ellington, *Music Is My Mistress*, p. 288.

8. Ibid.

9. CBS-TV film of the *Second Sacred Concert*, viewed at the Archives Center, NMAH, Smithsonian Institution.

10. Harvey, p. 11.

11. Gleason, *Celebrating the Duke*, p. 232.

12. Hoggard, Smithsonian program notes.

13. Ellington, with Dance, *Duke Ellington in Person: An Intimate Memoir,* p. 210.
14. Courtesy of the Archives Center, NMAH, Smithsonian Institution, but Ann K. Kuebler, archivist, believes that his handwriting is characteristic of early 1970s.

CHAPTER 10: CODA

1. Boyer, "The Hot Bach—II," reprinted in *The Duke Ellington Reader*, pp. 228–229.

BIBLIOGRAPHY

BOOKS

Budds, Michael J. *Jazz in the Sixties*. Iowa: University of Iowa Press, 1990.

Collier, James Lincoln. *Duke Ellington*. New York: Oxford University Press, 1987.

Cooke, Alistair. *Fun & Games with Alistair Cooke*. New York: Arcade Publishing, 1994.

Cone, James H. *The Spirituals and the Blues*. New York: Orbis, 1972.

Crouch, Stanley. *The All-American Skin Game, or, The Decoy of Race*. New York: Vintage Books, 1997.

Dance, Stanley. *The World of Duke Ellington*. New York: Charles Scribner's Sons, 1970.

Ellington, Duke. *Inspirational Music*. Miami Beach: Hansen House.

Ellington, Edward Kennedy. *Music Is My Mistress*. Garden City, New York: Doubleday & Company, Inc., 1973.

Ellington, Mercer, with Stanley Dance. *Duke Ellington in Person: An Intimate Memoir*. Boston: Houghton Mifflin, 1978.

Gabbard, Krin. *Jammin' at the Margins: Jazz and the American Cinema*. Chicago: The University of Chicago Press, 1996.

Gleason, Ralph J. *Celebrating the Duke* and Louis, Bessie, Billie, Bird, Carmen, Miles, Dizzy and Other Heroes. Boston: Little, Brown & Company, 1995.

Hajdu, David. *Lush Life: A Biography of Billy Strayhorn*. New York: Farrar Straus Giroux, 1996.

Harris, Michael W. *The Rise of Gospel Blues*. New York: Oxford University Press, Inc., 1992.

Hasse, John Edward. *Beyond Category: The Life and Genius of Duke Ellington*. New York: Simon & Schuster, 1993.

Hohenberg, John *The Pulitzer Diaries*. New York: Syracuse University Press, 1997.

Lambert, Eddie. *Duke Ellington: A Listener's Guide*. Copyright by Elaine Norsworthy. *Studies in Jazz Series*, No. 26, Institute of Jazz Studies, Rutgers, State University of New Jersey, gen. eds. Dan Morgenstern and Edward Berger. Maryland: Scarecrow Press, Inc., 1999.

Lewis, David Levering. *When Harlem Was in Vogue*. New York: Alfred A. Knopf, Inc., 1982.

Leonard, Neil. *Jazz, Myth and Religion*. New York: Oxford University Press, 1987.

Murray, Albert. *Stomping the Blues*. New York: Da Capo Press, 1976.

Ottley, Roi. *New World A-Coming*. New York: Arno Press and The New York Times, 1969.

Shapiro, Nat and Hentoff, Nat. *The Jazz Makers: Essays on the Greats of Jazz*. New York: Holt, Rhinehart and Winston, 1957.

Southern, Eileen. *The Music of Black Americans. A History, Third Edition*. New York: W.W. Norton & Company, Inc., 1983.

Tirro, Frank. Jazz: *A History, Second Edition*. New York: W.W. Norton & Company, Inc., 1993.

Tucker, Mark, ed. *The Duke Ellington Reader*. New York: Oxford University Press, Inc., 1993.

Tucker, Mark. *Ellington: The Early Years*. Illinois: University of Illinois Press, 1995.

Ulanov, Barry. *Duke Ellington*. New York: Creative Press, Inc., 1946.

By John Edward Hasse

Duke Ellington was captured in more than 10,000 recordings and it's easy for a consumer to feel bewildered by the hundreds of Ellington CDs now available.

As a starting point, I recommend *Beyond Category: The Musical Genius of Duke Ellington; His Greatest Victor, Bluebird, and RCA Recordings, 1927–67*, a 37-track, two-CD set issued by Smithsonian Recordings and BMG. I single out this anthology not because I produced and annotated the set, but because it's the most comprehensive single or double CD available, covering forty years of his music-making for the company that edges Columbia Records as having his greatest material.

Columbia Records, Ellington's other main label, has issued two valuable survey collections: *Reminiscing in Tempo* (Legacy) gathers material from the 1920s through the 1940s, including the entire *Reminiscing in Tempo* from 1935, as well as the 1958 Ellington-Mahalia Jackson recording of *Come Sunday*. Some Columbia highlights from 1956–1960 appear on *The Essential Duke Ellington* (CBS). Along with the *Beyond Category* set, these two Columbia discs provide a better overview of Ellington than any other four available discs.

Ellington's *Concert of Sacred Music* (the "First Sacred Concert") has been issued in two versions. The official, authorized version, recorded December 26, 1965, by RCA is available as *Duke Ellington's Concert of Sacred Music* (BMG France). A recording made of the work's premiere at Grace Episcopal Church, San Francisco, on September 16, 1965, has been issued by the British label Status as *Sacred Music: A Concert of Sacred Music from Grace Cathedral*. The *Second Sacred Concert* is available from Fantasy; two selections on the original LP release have been deleted to make it fit onto a single compact disc.

Black and Tan Fantasy, as well as the revival-tinged *Shout 'em, Aunt Tillie* can be heard on *Early Ellington, 1927–1934* (Bluebird). Studio versions of four excerpts from *Black, Brown, and Beige*, recorded in 1944, are included in the three-disc set *Black, Brown, and Beige* (RCA Bluebird). The version of *Black, Brown, and Beige* that features Mahalia Jackson is to be found on Columbia Records.

Other essential Ellington recordings include:

≠ *Swing 1930 to 1938* (ABC)
≠ *The Great Ellington Units* (RCA Bluebird)
≠ *The Blanton-Webster Band* (RCA Bluebird)
≠ *Ellington Uptown* (Columbia)
≠ *Piano Reflections* (Capitol)
≠ *Such Sweet Thunder* (Columbia)
≠ *Anatomy of a Murder* (Columbia)
≠ *The Far East Suite* (RCA Bluebird)
≠ *And His Mother Called Him Bill* (RCA Bluebird)
≠ *16 Most Requested Songs* (Columbia Legacy)

For those with deep pockets, there are two wide-ranging boxed sets. *Duke Ellington Anniversary* is a 13-disc set from the French label Masters of Jazz. Each disc is devoted to a theme, such as "Ballads," "Blues," "Dance," "Piano," "Portraits," and "Soloists."

The Godzilla of all jazz boxed sets is the 24-disc *Duke Ellington Centennial Edition* (BMG Music), which contains everything Ellington ever recorded for the RCA family of labels, including his *Concert of Sacred Music*, and the *Third Sacred Concert*. Through a licensing agreement with Fantasy Records, this set also puts the *Second Sacred Concert* together with the other two for the first time.

John Edward Hasse, author of *Beyond Category: The Life and Genius of Duke Ellington*, is Curator of American Music at the National Museum of American History, Smithsonian Institution.

INDEX